To John
A Good Fr
Keep on

Jack Stout

M000025719

TO HELL WITH TOGETHERNESS

THE STORY OF AN ALASKAN FAMILY
LIVING TOGETHER ON A REMOTE HOMESTEAD
WEST OF ANCHORAGE—1957-1962

JACK AND RITA STOUT

Enjoy
Rita Stout

Publication Consultants
Since 1978

PO Box 221974 Anchorage, Alaska 99522-1974
books@publicationconsultants.com
www.publicationconsultants.com

ISBN 978-0-9815193-4-0

Library of Congress Control Number: 2009931572

Photo Credits: Personal collection of author

Poetry Credit: *Sled Dog and Other Poems of the North*
by Charles E. Gillham
Standard Publications, Huntington, WV, 1950

Map Credit: Wikipedia, Alaska-Size.wpg, by Phizzy, copyright permis-
sion granted under GNU Free Documentation License

Cover photo: Taken by Jim Stout on his eighth birthday

seated (l-r): Joel and Jack Stout

standing (l-r): Mike, Butch, Rita Stout, and Joel Frazier

Printed in the United States of America

DEDICATION

Jack, Baldy, and Joel, thirty years later and thirty pounds heavier. Having these two as friends and neighbors may not be what made our homesteading possible, but they sure made our homesteading a lot easier and a lot more fun.

PREFACE

RITA

Between filing for our homestead on Bureau of Land Management (BLM) land in 1957 and the government granting of the patent in 1962, we spent five years on the homestead on Point MacKenzie in Southcentral Alaska. This point is across four and a half miles of water from Anchorage, yet the area is still remote and without road access. A boat made getting back and forth a possible commute. Other land was available for homesteading, but Jack selected this spot. Maybe he was looking for the Alaska of one's dreams.

Just doing what was required to keep on living on the homestead left little time to do the work that would improve our lifestyle. It took a day to go to town when it was necessary. It took another day to do the laundry. One day a week we spent cutting wood to keep warm, usually birch about five to six inches in diameter. The log was cut in lengths Jack could carry on his shoulder, then cut into stove lengths at the cabin. I helped to hold the log while it was being cut, then I shoved it through the "school marm" until a stove length was sticking out free. A school marm is a device with two legs sticking up to hold a log where it can be cut without getting an ax or saw into the dirt. Ours was a stump with two branches extending from the fork of the trunk. It kept the log from rolling when you didn't want it to. We set up our school marm high enough so Jack could cut two or three stove lengths before I had to extend some more. It also kept us from having to stop and stack the wood as often to get it out of the way. The name "school marm" was coined in the 1800s when some wag decided the device looked like a woman lying on her back with her legs up. The only woman you could count on being single in those days was the school teacher. Some people blamed the name on a logger, and some people claimed a cowboy was the culprit, but the name stuck. I have no idea why female teachers had to be single, but when Jack started school in the state of Washington in the '30s, that was still the rule.

Carrying a tree through a wild area with snow on the ground is neither easy nor fast. Each time we extended or moved the area where we were cutting firewood, everything was done on snowshoes. That's one reason Jack carried logs up to the cabin before they were cut into stove lengths. A log was anywhere up to sixteen feet in length, depending on diameter; the bigger the diameter, the heavier the log per foot. Carrying a log on your shoulder is hard work. Snowshoes multiply the effort needed. Once an area has been worked for a couple days, the snow has been packed and "set up" enough that snowshoes were no longer needed. We never clear-cut an area. The idea was to thin the trees, but leave enough of them to create a park-like setting.

We walked everywhere. We tied our kids to a packboard because no one had yet come out with a baby pack. The trail was too rough for wheels, so a stroller or wagon didn't work. Disposable diapers were not available, and with a baby less than a year old, we washed cloth diapers on a scrub board. Our grandparents worried about Indians; we worried about bears. When people talk about the good old days or preserving their culture when it involves lifestyle, I think they are crazy. I did it and, boy, am I happy to use a dishwasher, a vacuum, or a washer and dryer; whenever they are available—all things my grandparents didn't have. A furnace is not only cleaner than a wood stove, it provides heat without being tended at night. With natural gas, one never shovels coal.

Jack worked away from the homestead whenever he could so we had money to live on. This meant, at times, I was by myself with the kids. He also did all the shopping, because I couldn't. He walked from the cabin to the boat, two and a half miles, crossed the inlet and rushed about to catch the tide to again walk two and a half miles, this time with as many groceries as we could afford. Part of the afford was money, part weight, an important part was how long would it last without refrigeration, and how much water did it take to prepare the food.

The tide on Cook Inlet is the second highest in the world according to Guinness World Records, running forty feet several times per year. This is only second to the Bay of Fundy. The Bay of Fundy has very straight sides of granite while Cook Inlet has miles of tide flats, so, I believe, there is actually more water moving in Cook Inlet. It often goes from a minus five to a plus thirty-four, taking six hours to do so, and of course, every day high tide is at a different time. Trying to fit any other schedule around catching the tide is almost impossible, especially without a dock when you have to land on the beach.

Jack was stuck with all the heavy work, from cutting firewood to building shelter, and all of the hunting for the cook to put meat onto the table. For a while all of our water came from a spring on the beach. Jack walked the two and a half miles, filled the jerry can, and carried it back to the cabin. A jerry can of water weighs about fifty pounds. We had creeks and a swamp closer but that water was unsafe to drink. One gets "Beaver Fever" and may need a new kidney. I was glad to stay at the cabin to babysit.

People have made much progress since 1957. Things that are common today had not been heard of like cell phones, GPS systems, snowmobiles, and all-terrain vehicles. Items like these would have made our living so much different. We had no modern conveniences, nor could we get them; no electricity, no running water, no road access, therefore no truck or car to get things we needed. If you can imagine living on top of a mountain where all you have is what you carry, you can understand how we lived. Jack will tell you he knew every stump or tree where he could rest the weight of that pack he carried on his back.

It was when I was eight months pregnant and helping to dynamite a drainage ditch across a swamp that I decided to write a book and call it *To Hell With Togetherness*. I lived in a totally male environment. Games were wrestling or fighting with socks in the toe of other socks. Always lots of hungry males around. Fleshing a moose hide for tanning was free time activity.

This is a journal-like essay of those five years that Jack and I have written together and it is what we believe to be true. We thought we knew a lot about living, as most young people do, but, gad, did we have a lot to learn. I can't tell you why we did what we did, except once we got started, we were too stubborn to quit.

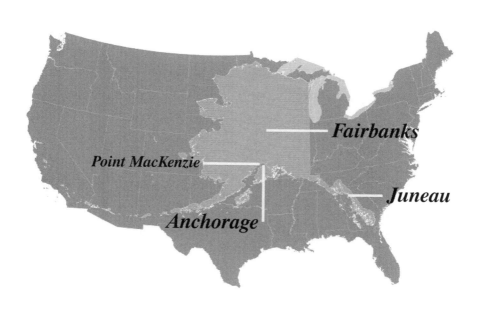

HOW BIG IS ALASKA?

Anchorage , Alaska, is now deposited appears that pursuant to the act of Congress of

and the acts supplemental thereto, the claim of   John Hiram Stout, Junior,

has been established and that the requirements of law pertaining to the claim have been met, for the following described land:

Seward Meridian, Alaska.

T. 14 N., R. 4 W.,

Sec. 32, NE¼.

The area described contains   160   acres, according to the official plat of the survey of the said land, on file in the Bureau of Land Management:

NOW KNOW YE, That the UNITED STATES OF AMERICA, in consideration of the premises, DOES HEREBY GRANT unto the said claimant   and to the heirs of the said claimant   the tract above described; TO HAVE AND TO HOLD the same, together with all the rights, privileges, immunities, and appurtenances, of whatsoever nature, thereunto belonging, unto the said claimant   and to the heirs and assigns of the said claimant   forever; subject to (1) any vested and accrued water rights for mining, agricultural, manufacturing, or other purposes, and rights to ditches and reservoirs used in connection with such water rights, as may be recognized and acknowledged by the local customs, laws, and decisions of courts; and (2) the reservation of a right-of-way for ditches or canals constructed by the authority of the United States, in accordance with the act of August 30, 1890 (26 Stat., 391, 43 U. S. C. sec. 945). There is also reserved to the United States a right-of-way for the construction of railroads, telegraph and telephone lines, in accordance with section 1 of the act of March 12, 1914 (38 Stat., 305, 48 U. S. C. sec. 305).
Excepting and reserving, also, to the United States all the oil and gas in the land so patented, and to it or persons authorized by it, the right to prospect for, mine, and remove such deposits from the same upon compliance with the conditions and subject to the provisions and limitations of the Act of March 8, 1922 (42 Stat. 415).
This entry is made under Section 29 of the Act of February 25, 1920 (41 Stat. 437) and the Act of March 4, 1933 (47 Stat. 1570) and the patent is issued subject to the rights of prior permittees or lessees to use so much of the surface of said land as is required for mining operations, without compensation to the patentee for damages resulting from proper mining operations.

IN TESTIMONY WHEREOF, the undersigned authorized officer of the Bureau of Land Management, in accordance with the provisions of the Act of June 17, 1948 (62 Stat., 476), has, in the name of the United States, caused these letters to be made Patent, and the Seal of the Bureau to be hereunto affixed.
GIVEN under my hand, in the District of Columbia, the THIRTIETH   day of   MARCH   in the year of our Lord one thousand nine hundred and   SIXTY-TWO and of the Independence of the United States the one hundred and   EIGHTY-SIXTH.

[SEAL]

FILED

For the Director, Bureau of Land Management.

By _Ruth W. Talley_

Chief, Patents Section.

Patent Number   1226026

U. S. GOVERNMENT PRINTING OFFICE   16—66812—6

THE COVETED PRIZE

This piece of paper granted us our "free land." The cost was lots of work and five years of our lives.

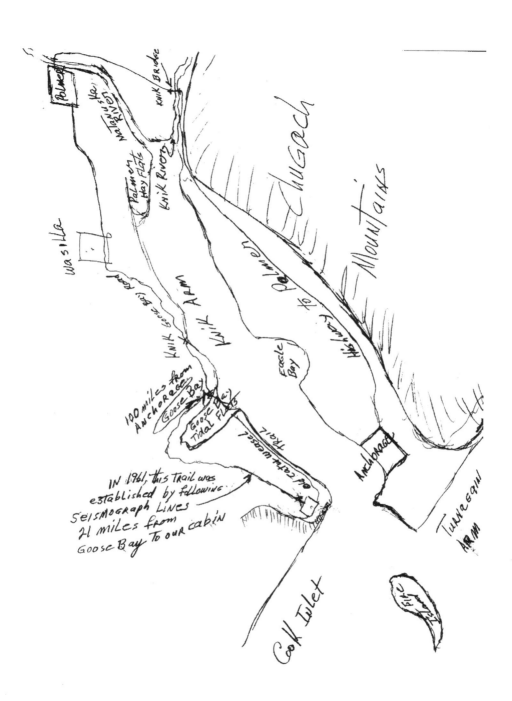

CHAPTER 1

JACK

It was a Wednesday evening in early May of 1954 when I got up from the table at our house in Los Angeles to answer the phone. My dad was calling from Anchorage. His first words were, "I've got a job for you if you can be here Sunday night and start work Monday." Talk about a bolt out of the blue! It was a job as a rear chainman on a survey crew. I had never done surveying, but I had grown up around heavy construction and both my dad and I knew I could do what was required to get the work done.

"How soon do I have to let you know?"

"Any time between now and six-thirty tomorrow morning."

"Give us a couple hours to figure this out and I'll call you back."

I wouldn't say I was excited, but I never did finish that dinner. I hung up and turned to my wife, Rita. "That was Pop. He has a job for me as soon as I can get to Alaska. What do you think? It won't wait until June." We talked it over. The obstacles were enormous: getting Rita settled into another place, selling the car, notifying my boss I am leaving, getting a jillion things packed and shipped, on and on into the night.

Rita was to graduate in June from the University of Southern California. While she didn't need to attend graduation, she did need to take finals in order to get her degree. That was a month away. We had an eighteen-month-old son and she didn't drive. We were living in an apartment-type row house in Los Angeles and had stuff like cribs and clothing to deal with, and this job needed a person in a week's time.

Rita and I were twenty-two. We met in Los Angeles before my folks had moved to Alaska. I had decided to stay with her until she graduated from college and then we were planning to migrate north. She had a job offer to teach in Anchorage the following

September. We talked about different ways to travel all the time, but now we had to make decisions quickly.

After a few more phone calls and lots of checking, we decided that I would take the baby and fly to Alaska and stay with my folks until Rita got there. My mother would babysit and get to know her only grandson. We would pack things to ship and give away the rest. Rita would stay in Los Angeles until graduation and leave the next day to fly north. This way I could get to Anchorage in time to take the job and Rita could finish school. The next few days were hectic.

Our firstborn son, Butch, and I left Los Angeles on Saturday night at eleven p.m. in a DC 6, a very modern prop plane. It could fly for twelve hours and still have a safe reserve of fuel. It would take six hours or so to reach Seattle and another six to reach Anchorage. Today's jets take three hours to Anchorage from Seattle, and there is nonstop service from many major cities. Other differences include the lack of room in the seats today, and the smaller meals that almost fill you up. The stewardess is now too busy selling drinks to visit, and the uniform of the day for the traveler is a pair of blue jeans instead of a suit. No woman wears a girdle anymore, and men wear either a baseball cap or a cowboy Stetson.

Upon our arrival in Seattle, we were both hungry after our first leg of the flight, so we took the elevator to the third floor to the restaurant. It wasn't open yet. Try telling a hungry eighteen-month-old that breakfast would have to wait. Actually, Butch was pretty good about it. I took him for a ride on the elevator. He'd learned about elevators in Los Angeles on an express elevator in a high-rise building and knew what the buttons were. We rode with whomever got on that elevator for a while. We'd gotten to the first floor for the third time, and I took him by the hand and walked off the elevator. Butch suddenly snatched his hand away and darted back onto the elevator. I'd been up for a little better than twenty-four hours, and my reaction time was off. I got turned around just in time to see the elevator door close as Butch was waving bye-bye. I tore madly up the stairs and got to the second floor just in time to see that same door close with that little stinker still inside. Third floor, same story. Back down to the second again! Down to the first. I came around the corner and some guy's standing there holding Butch by the hand. He started to roar with laughter as I came into view. That's probably what saved Butch's life. Until that guy started laughing, I hadn't seen any humor in the situation.

We finally got something to eat and afterward I bought a big low-pressure ball for him to play with. Butch could get his arms around it just enough to pick it up. I played catch with him for a few minutes and fell asleep. I awoke a short time later (I think). Butch was entertaining himself with the ball—throwing it at people to tease them. The rest of that four-hour layover was a blur. Finally we boarded the plane and flew on to Anchorage, arriving at two o'clock Sunday afternoon. It was a very long day.

The plane pulled up on the tarmac and the pilot shut down the engines. The stairs were rolled up to the plane and people started filing off. I stepped out onto the platform at the top of the stairs and was aware of two things: Mom and Pop were at the foot of those stairs waving at us, and out over everything, I saw the Chugach Mountains. I waved back at the folks and fell in love with those mountains. I've never gotten over my love of those mountains.

RITA

Jack and I met in 1950 and married in 1951. Jack had worked to put me through school. John, or Butch as he was called back then, was born in 1952. I had been in Los Angeles for ten years. Jack had been there about eight years. Los Angeles was growing, getting crowded and smoggier. We knew we didn't want to stay there after I graduated. My graduation was important enough for

3

us to stick to that plan. My dad died when I was two and I was raised knowing that a woman never knew when she would have to support her family, and an education was the key to that support. I was studying to be a teacher. The only university in Alaska was in Fairbanks. Jack's folks were very happy in Anchorage and wanted us to join them. We knew nothing about Fairbanks.

I arrived in Anchorage a month later than Jack. He and his folks and Butch met me at the plane. Jack had a dozen red roses in his hand. I knew roses were expensive, but I was one of the few graduates who didn't get a gift from the love of their life the day before. Nancy got pearls from a boyfriend from Korea, but me, nothing from a husband. I had been both hurt and embarrassed. Now, where no one could see, he had American Beauties for me. I also got to share the news that, yes, I was pregnant, which meant no teaching that year so Jack alone would have to support us again.

My first thoughts about Alaska included things like, where are the trees? I expected the tall redwoods of Oregon and California. Instead I got short, scraggly spruce. The weather was a delightful surprise. It was warm and sunny. The mountains were breathtaking.

After years in California, the price of fresh vegetables was astonishing. The ingredients for a tossed green salad cost ten bucks. Eggs were old and expensive, and forget dried cereal. Refrigerated cargo containers were still years away, and bulky items were sent by the space they took up rather than weight, so toilet paper and paper towels were also expensive.

CHAPTER 2

RITA

We found a little two-room house in the Bootleggers Cove area near downtown Anchorage with an oil cook range that heated the house and the hot water in a coil within the firebox. The coil was connected to a hot-water tank. One lit the stove by turning on the oil flow, waiting until there was about a half cup of oil in the burner box, and then using a piece of paper for kindling and a match to start the oil burning. This was number two diesel oil stored in three fifty-five gallon barrels on a rack outside the house. The oven on this stove never got hot enough to bake potatoes, and biscuits had to be turned over to brown on the other side. Actually, this house consisted of two one-room cabins shoved together. The bathroom had a curtain for a door. The cabin was on the back of a lot with another two-room cabin on the front. The bedroom was large enough for a double bed, a crib, and a cot. We had a deep closet, but I don't remember any drawers. The other part was a combination living room/kitchen. We had a table and chairs, a couch, a rocker, and the usual kitchen. Both cabins had a door to the outside.

JACK

We were in a neighborhood of old sourdoughs, a group of bachelors in their late seventies and eighties. There are a number of definitions of the term sourdough when talking about a person. One was "someone who has turned sour on Alaska and hasn't enough dough to get out." The most popular was, "a guy who's wintered out at least one year, has peed in the Yukon River, killed a grizzly, and slept with a squaw." To those old men it was someone who'd wintered out enough times to prove he could handle anything the Arctic could throw at them. When they felt "you'd do to ride the river with," you were invited into a closed society of very tough, rugged individuals.

These men each lived alone in one-room log cabins. They cut wood all summer to heat their places in the winter. They each had a garden for potatoes and peas. They shared a retired sixty-year-old prostitute who had a driver's license, and they bought her a car so she could take them rabbit hunting or berry picking. These guys came into the North Country before cars were invented. They could mush a dog team, run a boat, drive and ride horses, even fly an airplane, but most of them had never learned to drive a car. Their lifestyle didn't include a need for a car. They spent all their time in the Bush, mining or trapping or commercial fishing. They came to town now and then to settle up with suppliers, get drunk, and get laid. If they needed a car while in town, they hired a cab.

When Rita and I got to the territory, getting a driver's license had very few restrictions. You had to be at least sixteen and have three dollars. You could renew your driver's license after your seventieth birthday, but you couldn't buy your first license if you were seventy or older, and these guys were that age or older when they moved to town.

RITA

It was a very interesting neighborhood. The men ignored Jack and me. They had all been in Alaska since the gold rush of '98 and we were just kids, and newcomers besides. They called Tom, our landlord, "that young fellow across the street." He was sixty-four. He was also a "Johnny-come-lately"—he hadn't come to Alaska until '32. The old guys looked down their noses at Tom because he wouldn't live their "wild-ass" lifestyle. He never went uptown and got drunk. He put all his money into real estate and was quite wealthy. Still, Tom was kind of the leader of the neighborhood. He kept things straight, and it was Tom that people came to when there was more trouble than they could handle.

The retired prostitute had previously had cancer, so Tom loaned her a cabin to live in. She drank like a fish and bragged about the tube of garlic paste that she carried in her glove compartment.

She planned that if the police stopped her, she would shoot a gob of this paste into her mouth. The smell of the garlic was supposed to keep the cop from smelling whatever she had been drinking and protect her from a DUI.

JACK

Tom, our landlord, was a big game guide. One hunt I remember was for the New York Museum of Natural History. They were collecting animals for dioramas. Another hunt was three men for thirty days. They were to harvest each of the five big game animals of Alaska: bear, moose, caribou, goat, and sheep. This hunt involved having established camps for each hunt and moving the whole hunting party to each camp. In those days, a hunt like that cost about ten thousand dollars. I have no idea what it would cost today.

Tom and I became good friends and we'd spend quite a bit of time visiting when he was in town. I was at his house next door to ours one evening and he was telling me about his most recent hunt. Suddenly his front door slammed open and the retired prostitute came bursting in.

"Tom! Tom! you've got to stop those old fools; they're going to kill each other!" Tom got her calmed down enough to be reasonably coherent. She'd gotten the day of the week confused and ended up in the wrong cabin. When the guy she was supposed to be with found her, she was already involved with the wrong guy. An angry argument ensued. In the heat of the moment, things were said that couldn't be taken back and could only be settled with guns.

When Tom and I got out there, one old guy was standing at the end of an alley, under a streetlight, leaning on his rifle. We went to him, and Tom tried talking sense to him. He just ignored us and continued staring down the alley. Tom turned to me, "I'm going down to Erickson's and see if I can talk sense into him. If he comes out without me, knock this idiot down and then run." With that he walked away, toward Erickson's cabin. I watched him disappear. I turned so that I could keep my eye on the old man and Erickson's cabin. I was wondering why the ground couldn't just open up and swallow me. I said something to him. I don't even remember what it was, but it was as though I wasn't even there.

Finally, a century or so later, Tom came out alone. I think I proved that a person can hold his breath for fifty years and not even turn blue. Tom came up to us. "Fifty years of friendship means more to him than it does to you!" He turned to me, "Let's go finish our conversation." I wondered for years if I'd really had the nerve to take a swing at that old guy.

I keep saying "old," but these men weren't old. They seemed old to us. When you're twenty-two, anybody over forty seems old. They were aged, but not old. They still lived just like they had lived fifty years before. They were still straight and strong and fiercely independent. They stacked their firewood along the outside walls of their cabins. That kept it under the eaves but, more importantly, it added extra insulation to the walls. Through the winter they always brought their wood stack down evenly so they didn't get a cold spot on the wall. One day, I noticed Erickson stacking some of his wood. It looked like about two cords or so. A cord is a stack of wood two feet high, two feet wide, and eight feet long. I had to pretend that I was looking for something to do to keep me out of the house.

"Mr. Erickson, my wife is cleaning house. I need an excuse to stay out of there or I'll be moving furniture all afternoon. If I could help you with this wood, I'd sure appreciate it." He stopped and straightened his back to get a kink out, spit some snoose while he was deciding if I could help or not.

"Needs to be stacked good and tight."

"Yes sir."

"Well, I guess us men have to stick together on that house cleanin' stuff."

"We sure do."

8

"Okay, maybe the two of us can get it all stacked today. First name's Robert."

"I'm Jack."

"What brought you to Alaska?"

"Getting the hell away from Los Angeles! I wanted to live where I could raise boys in a way that would teach them to be men."

Not much else was said for the next two hours.

We were just finishing the last of the wood when Erickson said, "I'm going over to Gunnar's for a drink. Come on along and I'll talk him into letting you have one, too." Gunnar's cabin was just beyond the next one. I followed Erickson through the door. There were eight people in the room already. The chairs and the edge of the bed were occupied. Erickson pointed over his shoulder at me, "This is the kid from across the street. His name is Jack."

As he said this, he walked over and squatted against the wall. I nodded hello to everyone and hunkered down beside Erickson. The bottle was passed to us. Erickson took a hit and passed it to me. Everyone watched to see how I handled that. I didn't wipe off the top, I just put it to my mouth and took a big swallow. I managed not to cough or get tears in my eyes. After that, when the bottle came by me, I put my tongue over it and bobbed my Adam's apple up and down as if I was drinking. Once the bottle came to me almost empty. I had to "kill it" and get another bottle. A little explanation here: by the time men quit coming in, there were thirteen of us. There was half a case of booze in the center of the floor. When you finished a bottle, you got another, pulled the cork, and started it around. Everyone drank straight from the bottle.

Pretty soon the stories got started. Many of them were memories of places and times. Some of them were pure yarn, but we all treated them as fact. It was legal to top a yarn. I wish I'd had a tape recorder in there. I was there about three hours and I would have had one hundred years of stories. Much of what I heard was an actual history of Alaska that never made it into any books. This is the only story I can remember. Moose and caribou can easily outrun any of the hunting animals if they get a chance. But these guys were talking about swiftness in relation to getting off the mark. One guy was sure that the lynx was the quickest of them all. This is the story he told to back up his claim.

"I had a lynx almost get me with my own bullet once." That got everyone's attention. He took a pull on the bottle. He passed the bottle and, glancing around, went on with his story. "Some o' you been on my trapline. Ya ever notice the bullet hole in the doorjamb? Well, I'd got the dogs hooked up and gone back in the cabin for my rifle and my grub bag. I come back out and, by gar, dere's a lynx sitting under the spruce tree I keep my meat hanging in. He opened his mouth and yowled at me. He did that twice. I put down my grub bag and raised my rifle. He opened his mouth again and I pulled the trigger. I put a round right down his gullet. Now, that wily ol' cat suckered me right in. He knew I'd do that if he provoked me enough. Sure enough, he swapped ends so fast that when that damned bullet come out the other end, it came right at me. But my aim was truer than his. I got his pelt, but he got the doorjamb right behind my head." Nobody even smiled. But no one tried to top him.

I wish I could tell you what my afternoon with those men meant to me. I was drinking with giants! These men had each spent fifty years in the Arctic. They had taken everything the Arctic had thrown at them and, not only survived, they'd thrived! They'd faced storms on land and water, bears, cold, life-threatening injuries, plane crashes, having to walk out because transportation failed—if Murphy thought of it, Murphy threw it at them. In a way, everything I did in that cabin that afternoon was a test. They watched me. To some degree, they accepted me. It was one of the most enthralling afternoons of my life.

One of those guys had an old-fashioned concertina. It was red, octagon-shaped, and had a few buttons on one end. He'd get a little juiced up, just enough to take care of the "rheumatiz," and start pumping that thing. He played what we used to call barn dance music. He could make that thing sing. In the middle of winter he'd get going, and windows would go up all over the neighborhood. There was no way you could keep your feet from moving when he got warmed up.

Every now and then these guys would go uptown, about ten blocks, and get rip-roaring drunk. They had to. It was tradition. People expected it of them. They were "He-Men of the North!" One day Rita and I watched three of them come home from one such expedition. They were walking in the street; well, staggering's probably a better description. In those days the streets in most parts of town were dirt, without sidewalks. These guys were wandering back and forth across the street from the grass line on one side to the grass line on the other. They were so fixed on their attempt at navigation that I doubt they were aware of anything that did not actually impede their progress. Two of them were leaning into the one in the center. They kept him more or less vertical, and so it was up to him to steer them home.

He did keep them in the street, but just barely. He made all the turns as needed so they were headed in the right direction. They finally made it to his cabin. They had to go to his, because he was the only one vertical enough to hit the keyhole. They got to his front door and got him standing as tall as possible. He started stabbing at the keyhole with a big, old-fashioned skeleton key. Now here's the rub. When they weren't moving, they started sagging. When the key was below the keyhole, he stopped stabbing, and they all worked their way back to their approximation of vertical. They went through this ritual several times, and he finally got the key in. They all disappeared inside. I guess they all lay across the bed to sleep it off. These guys all talked about moving to the Pioneer Home the next year. As far as I know, none of them ever made it. Today, there's only one of the cabins standing. The rest have been torn down, and multi-story condos and high-rise apartments were built on the land.

Last of the original homes/cabins in modern-day Bootleggers Cove in Anchorage. Condo development has taken over the entire area. Our first home in Anchorage was similar to this "last standing soldier."

CHAPTER 3

RITA

The military has played a big part in the development of Anchorage and the surrounding areas. Establishing two bases, Elmendorf Air Force Base and Fort Richardson Army Post, meant civilian jobs with the money it brought to a community and its people. There was not enough base housing, so many GI families lived off base, including the young couple who lived on the other half of our lot. Jack's dad was working on the new military hospital as an inspector for the Corp of Engineers. Jack was to work on a survey crew putting in roads, steam lines, or any other facilities needed to service the new hospital.

Jack worked construction as long as the job lasted. Construction shut down when the ground froze. After that Jack drove a cab. People took whatever jobs they could find. Going to work for the city as a garbage truck driver was a good job because it was steady. Most of the jobs were seasonal: fishing or construction. Many people lived on unemployment insurance, but Jack had to draw unemployment from California, which wasn't enough money for us to pay our rent of ninety dollars a month. Jack worked a twelve-hour shift, from six p.m. to six a.m. I would stay up as late as I could so I could sleep late and keep the house quiet for Jack to sleep. I read a great deal.

At that time Anchorage had thirteen thousand people, unpaved streets, and two stop lights. You rode a cab by area. If you stayed in area one, the fare was a buck. To cross into another area, the fare was two bucks. The bus was so slow and came by so rarely that everyone used a cab. Up until we got to Alaska, Jack's folks had not had a car. A whole lot of what is now the Municipality of Anchorage was not part of Anchorage back then. Spenard, Mountain View, and Eastchester were separate public utility districts with different governments, volunteer fire departments, and territorial troopers for police service. Spenard even had its own library.

The school district was the Greater Anchorage Area School District and covered the whole area. The new high school just being built is now known as West High School. The federal impact was so great that there was a lot of money to spend on schools where GI families were in attendance, so this school ended up with an auditorium that would seat two thousand people.

The orchestra pit was an unusual thing to have in a high school auditorium. It raised and lowered like an elevator. The musicians would take their places while the pit was in the basement, then it would be raised into place. The stage revolved. You could set up or remove props on the back half and revolve the stage between scenes or acts. At the time of construction, there was only one other theater with this system in the whole USA. The West High auditorium was used for many civic activities, including the Bob Hope Christmas Show for the troops.

People wore GI surplus clothing or fur all winter. There was a long green parka that was very popular with both men and women. Everyone looked alike. All the kids had parkas from Sears: red, blue, gray, or khaki. The kids wore flannel-lined jeans over long johns to school. In the summer, one was expected to dress up. Ladies' hats and white gloves were not uncommon. I went into a department store in clean, ironed pedal pushers and a white blouse. No one would wait on me. Women would come into town from the suburbs all dressed up. They were driving Jeeps with double-wide tires chained up to get through the mud. Before they left their vehicles they changed from their mud boots into high-heeled shoes. Men often wore an Alaskan tuxedo, a gray twill-like pants and jacket. Bolo ties and watchbands were decorated with gold nuggets. No one shined their shoes.

That first winter was an education for us both. We had never lived in snow country. The weather was colder and winter was longer than any winter either of us had ever faced. I had been in Southern California since I was six, where thirty-two degrees meant the ranchers used smudge pots to protect fruit trees, and a warm sweater meant winter gear. Flowers bloomed all year, and we had outdoor PE class at school in shorts at eight a.m. Now I needed a scarf to protect not only my face but my lungs, a hat for my ears, and gloves or mittens.

I was used to life in a major city. Los Angeles had major department stores downtown and public transportation was available. There was a population of a couple of million people. I attended a three-year high school of five thousand students. In Anchorage, there was the Northern Commercial Company on Fourth Avenue. It sold everything from clothes and food to Caterpillar tractors, commonly called bulldozers, all in the same store. There were lots of bars, two movie theaters, and a five-and-ten-cent store. There were dress shops and a place to buy women's hats. The main street had a sporting goods store that sold lots of rifles. The Elks Club had its own building with an open room that was used for dances and the Little Theater plays. The buildings that survived the 1964 quake are still in use. The 4th Avenue Theater, with its beautiful mural and stars on the ceiling, is now a souvenir shop. The old city hall is now a museum, as the new city offices take up an eight-story building. Most of the businesses downtown are now involved with tourism.

JACK

Another thing we were constantly running into was strictly cultural. Length of residence was a status symbol. "I'm no cheechako. I've been here five years" (or fifty years or whatever). No one was unfriendly— they just were not going to accept us into the culture until we'd been here through at least one winter. If we'd needed help, someone would have stepped up, but they'd have watched us more closely to see if we could cope. People were always ranked according to when they got here. The epitome of that was brought home to me in the late sixties. I was talking to

15

an old man who'd come to Alaska to work summers each year until he finished college. He moved North the day after graduation and never looked back. We were talking about a specific gold mining area. When I mentioned a historical "fact," Ralph corrected me and told me what really happened.

I said, "I'm sure not going to debate you on that, but that's what Arnie told me."

"Oh hell," said Ralph, "He didn't even get here 'til '04! He doesn't know!"

RITA

Mike, our second son, was born in January of 1955. I went to work the next fall teaching third grade at Woodland Park School in Spenard. With both of us working, I had to learn to drive. There were times when Jack was out of town working and my school was about three miles from where we lived. The kids were at separate babysitters so I had to get them home and back the next morning as well as get to work. That year and most of the years after, when construction shut down, Jack was our babysitter. Our kids had Mommy from June to September, Daddy from October to April, and a babysitter the rest of the year.

JACK

I started teaching Rita to drive as soon as the streets got slippery. I didn't want her to have a whole summer to get used to the idea that stepping on the brake would always get you out of trouble. Our three-year-old actually knew more about driving than Rita did. When Rita made a mistake, he would tease her. It didn't take long to decide that he should visit Grandmom while Rita was taking her driving lessons.

All cars had six-volt batteries. Head bolt heaters helped to get the car started on winter mornings, but there were times during the day when people started their cars every two hours to let the engine warm up so it would start again later in the day. People

16

carried two sets of keys. You would go to the grocery store, lock the car with the motor running, do your shopping, and come back to a warm car. Other more trusting people just left the motor running while they shopped.

That second winter we had a record snowfall: one hundred seventy-one inches with forty-seven in one dump, followed by a three-day windstorm a week later. In all of our years here, this was the only time I have seen the town shut down because of snow. It took bulldozers to open our street again. We had no snow on one side of the house and could step up on the roof on the other. The clotheslines were about a foot above the snow. One of our neighbors actually got snowed in when the snow blocked their door. They pushed their little boy of three or four out the door over the top of the drift. He slid down to the ground and came to our house for help to dig the rest of the family out.

RITA
Jack worked that summer on the Aleutian Chain—good money, lots of overtime, but totally remote—so we saved our money, bought a small house on what was then Campbell Station Road. Today, it is West Tudor and the house would be in the center of the road if it still existed. We worked at raising our family. We were looking forward to, and working for, a better future.

Our little two room cabin in Bootleggers Cove the morning after the wind storm that followed a record snow dump in 1955. The black is the snow that was packed up against the door. One garbage can has no snow under half of it. In places one could step over the clothes line. Our neighbor's house is about the same size as ours.

CHAPTER 4

RITA

The requirements for homesteading were established in 1862 when the railroad and the government were working to settle the West. A man could file on one hundred sixty acres of government land, build a habitable dwelling, live there for seven months out of the year for three consecutive years, clear and plant a crop of something other than native grass, and then in title the land became his. The requirements were established at a period in American history when women, especially married women, really didn't count. Everything to do with the homestead was in the man's name, and it was he who had to establish residence. If his wife was there, he could be somewhere else working, as the homestead was then his family home. By now, most homesteaders were really not interested in becoming farmers, and the land available wasn't really farmland, but it was a good way to get the land on the tax rolls.

Jack's grandfather had helped people settle on homesteads in Kansas right after the Civil War, and Jack had grown up on the stories of his grandfather and how the man had gotten rich. With this family history, I think the day Jack landed in Anchorage he decided he wanted to go homesteading. He looked around and he talked to others and he dreamed. There was still a lot of land available. The first three years I was teaching, I had a coworker who was married to a guy who also was into "homesteading." Dave had a homestead and a fish site on Point MacKenzie.

Jack became interested in Point MacKenzie, across Knik Arm from Anchorage. Knik Arm is an extension of Cook Inlet, a body of water extending from the Pacific Ocean inland for two hundred miles. The inlet splits into two arms just below Anchorage. Those two arms are Turnagain Arm, named by Captain Cook when he had to "turn around again" while searching for the Northwest

Passage, and Knik Arm that forces saltwater up to the mouth of the Knik River. As it passes Anchorage, Knik Arm is four and one-half miles wide. The tide on this body of water is the second highest range in the world. There is no bridge across the arm and by land there were one hundred twenty miles of road from Anchorage north through Palmer and around Knik Arm to Goose Bay, and then twenty-one miles of virgin timberland, so in effect there was no road access of any kind to the point.

This lack of transportation was an obstacle in the settlement of Point MacKenzie. At the time we started homesteading and before, everything went into this area by water. There were boating people with summer getaways on the beach. Many of them talked about someday retiring to their cabin. Dave had a vision of a community near his land and was interested in finding others to bring it about. He had told so many about the area that there were about a dozen interested. Everyone knew that someday a causeway would be built across Knik Arm to provide an extension to the land used by Anchorage, and logically that causeway would land somewhere near Point MacKenzie, so someday there would be a community in the area. Anchorage had mountains, water, and two military bases as boundaries, so across the inlet was the only direction for growth.

Jack was working with Joel Frazier up on a mountain above Ski Bowl, a recreation site in the Chugach Mountains east of Anchorage. They were surveying for a Nike site. Nike was an aircraft defense system before ICBMs (Intercontinental Ballistic Missiles, an early Star Wars type of defense system). While eating lunch one day, they were looking at the view and discussing homesteading and Jack told Joel about Dave. The two decided to go across the inlet and look at what land was available.

The federal government had established a gunnery impact range for Elmendorf Air Force Base. There were only twelve and a half square miles of land available to homesteading adjacent to and on the south side of the gunnery range. This land included Point

MacKenzie. It was these twelve and a half square miles that were the topic of discussion that day.

Dave took Jack and Joel across the inlet in his boat and they all walked back to an area where there were two homestead sites available. The land looked okay, so Joel and Jack tossed a coin to see who got what parcel. Dave promised to help with transportation, and he also introduced Jack and Joel to Baldy, another man who was interested in land in the area. The year was 1957. First there was a trip to the land office. Jack filed on one hundred sixty acres of land near Point MacKenzie. Jack and Joel claimed land two and a half miles from the beach. Their homesteads were between six and seven miles from downtown Anchorage in a straight line. But their land, only that six miles from downtown Anchorage, was in an absolutely primeval forest full of bears, wolves, moose, and all other creatures indigenous to this part of Alaska. The parcel Jack selected was half good high ground and half muskeg swamp. The high ground had birch, spruce, cottonwood, and alder. There were fiddlehead fern, iris, wild roses, and many kinds of berries. The swamp had streams flowing under grass and plants that like having wet feet. In some places one could walk easily, other spots one would sink chest deep in cold water and muck.

Many things prompted Jack's choice to take land in this area. One was its proximity to Anchorage by boat; another, the dreams and plans of putting a causeway across the arm to open this land and to provide land for Anchorage to grow onto. Both Joel and Jack believed that anyone having title to land over there could make a nice profit if and when the causeway happened. Being close to Anchorage (by boat it was about half an hour) where our homes and jobs were meant we could spend more time on the land and still work. Another factor that prompted this decision was probably the fact that the land was off the beaten path. While many people homesteaded near the highway, that wasn't as romantic or adventurous as being out in the woods. The land office approved the filing on July 22, 1957. Now all Jack had to do was "prove up," meet the requirements established by the BLM in order to claim the land as his.

According to the local BLM office, Jack had five years to move on, build a habitable dwelling, clear one-eighth of the land, and plant a crop. To go by their time schedule, he was to move on within five months because the residency was to be within the first three years. I was pregnant, expecting our third child. We had two boys, two and four, and Jet, our dog, a coal black miniature cocker spaniel. I had signed a teaching contract for the 1957-58 school year. So, along about December, Jack filed for a time extension on establishing residence.

CHAPTER 5

JACK

I spent the fall on "the other side" helping Joel, Roy, (better known as Baldy), and Ray get their cabins up. The four of us devised a plan. We would all work together building our respective cabins. First, we'd build Baldy's, then Ray's, then Joel's, then ours.

Rita and I didn't intend to "move on" until late June the next summer, so our cabin wasn't so pushed for time. The others wanted to have their cabins up in time to "winter" in them. We'd build Baldy's and stay in it while we did the others. Now all we had to do was get the building material over and set the plan in motion.

Getting the material there was a greater task logistically than building the cabins would be. Everything had to be transported by water across Knik Arm. The tidal range is such that everything is planned around where the water will be at a given time. We were using a dory, a flat-bottomed, twenty-two foot open boat.

We'd set the boat so that it would "go dry" about an hour after high tide. This gave us ten to twelve hours to get a load of building material from the lumberyard, load it into the boat, and be ready to go when the boat floated once again. Then we'd run it across the inlet and unload it. Actually, we tried to get two trips in per tide. Then all we had to do was get all the stuff to the top of a ninety-foot-high bluff and back to the building sites.

It took only a few trips from the beach, up a cut in the bluff, and half a mile back to Baldy's building site with a bunch of lumber on our shoulders, to realize that some mechanical help on the toting would be really, really nice.

Dave, Baldy, and I were at Baldy's cabin site when Baldy said, "A Jeep would work. I know a friend who has one but I can't bring it over because he's behind on payments and he's promised to take it in to the finance company."

I asked him, "How much does he owe?"

"I'm not sure, but there's a little over two years' payments at one hundred thirty-five dollars a month."

"Well, why don't you and I go see him and see what we can work out?"

Dave was there at this time and he said, "I know a fellow that can weld up some rims so we can dual up all the way around, and with chains that would help in getting across the swamps."

The three of us decided to go to town right then. We walked down to the beach and Dave's boat. The boat was high and dry because the ebbing tide had left it stranded.

The only way for us to get to the water was to make our way across the mud to the boat, and then skid it down to the water. You don't walk on this mud. You slide your feet along as if wearing cross-country skis. If you're lucky, you don't get a foot stuck. If you're a little unlucky, one foot might get slightly stuck, but you can get it unstuck without losing your boot. A little worse luck and you lose one or both boots.

There have been a few times in recent history when someone's luck was so bad that they were still stuck thigh deep when the tide came back. No one has ever survived that.

Baldy, Dave, and I got to the boat. We worked it loose in the mud and got it sliding to the water. We were all able to jump in without leaving any boots behind and headed to Anchorage.

We "landed" the boat in Bootleggers Cove. The story goes that during prohibition, "moonshiners" from the Susitna River Valley brought their product, Susitna Dew, into Anchorage for sale. They couldn't take illegal liquor into Ship Creek, so they smuggled it into Anchorage through Bootleggers Cove.

The mud in the cove, on the Anchorage side, is a long, gradual slope from wherever the water is, up to the sand that starts at the high-water mark. One "lands" a boat by going lickety-split toward

Summer and the low tide mud flats—looking west from Anchorage.
Arrow points to our haul-out cut in the 90-foot-high bluff.

the beach. Baldy, Dave, and I all got onto the beach as fast as the boat would go. At the last second, Dave yanked the outboard shaft up out of the water and shut the engine off. The boat slid quite a ways up the slope. As it stopped, everybody jumped out. Baldy and Dave held the boat to keep it from sliding back out toward the water. I grabbed the anchor and, dragging the anchor rope, skied as fast as I could toward the beach. When I came to the end of the rope, I "set the hook" by stomping the anchor into the mud. Hopefully, the next high tide would float the boat right up to the beach.

We three went our respective ways. Baldy said he'd call the guy with the Jeep and the finance guy and try to set up an appointment. Then he'd call me at home and we'd go see him. I went home to discuss with Rita why we needed to buy a Jeep. A short time later, Baldy called and said we could go in anytime.

We met with the owner of the finance office. His name was Tom Fink, a man who would someday be mayor of Anchorage and run for governor of Alaska, a state that didn't even exist yet. Tom and I put together a deal. I had to pay off the principal of the existing note. He felt that the interest he'd gotten to date was a reasonable profit, and we cleared the book of a bad debt. I wrote him a check and he signed over the title. As simple as that. It took a few days to get the Jeep rigged with dual tires all the way around. Now all we had to do was get it across the inlet.

We set two dories side by side about four feet apart, as close to the beach as possible. Then we connected them by lashing four-by-fours across them. Each timber was long enough to be lashed to both gunwales of each dory and span the distance between the two. Next, we nailed plywood over the timbers to create a deck for the Jeep. We also used planks and plywood to create a ramp and drove the Jeep up onto the dories. We picked up the ramp material and loaded it onto the deck beside the Jeep. All we had to do now was wait for the next tide and pray that it would be flat calm. We weren't exactly set to handle a storm at sea. The next tide floated us as gently as we'd prayed, and we eased across the inlet and disembarked our rolling stock. We dismantled our "catamaran" and hauled the lumber to the top of the bluff and back to Baldy's.

Roy's cabin—where we were penned in by a bear most of a day and where I threw dishwater in the bear's face.

Our good friend Roy ("Baldy") relaxing in his cabin

Roy, facing camera, and Jack in Roy's cabin in the winter of 1957

The Four Men of Point McKenzie
from l-r: Jack (standing), Ray Roach, Roy "Baldy" Baldwin, Joel Frazier plus Hilma Baldwin, Roy's mother—winter of 1957-1958.

28

CHAPTER 6

JACK

We four guys worked on the cabins and roads during the day. We used the Jeep to pull down trees to create a trail wide enough for the Jeep. Someone drove up close to the tree and, standing on the Jeep, attached a chain as high as he could reach. Then he backed up, pulling the tree out of the ground. The Jeep didn't have a top on it and sometimes the tree was taller than the chain was long. On these occasions, the guy driving the Jeep might get a pretty good thumping. During the winter when the swamp was frozen, we could go all over and put in these trails. We also got the building materials across the swamp to build Joel's and our cabin.

One winter day, Joel and I were working together at his place. We worked all day in the cold and finally went back to Baldy's cabin. Baldy was in town, so we walked into a cold cabin. We got a fire going in the barrel stove. Baldy had a thermometer outside one window set so it could be read from inside. It read five degrees above zero. We did a few chores and the cabin warmed up enough to take off our coats and start fixing dinner. Joel checked the thermometer again. "What did you say the temp was when we got here?"

"Five above."

"Well, it's twenty-four above now." We got dinner ready and sat down to eat. Joel was doing the dishes when I happened to look out the window. "Holy Cow! It's thirty-six degrees out there!" The swamp we had to get all our building material across had been frozen enough to drive on for only two days. We were having a Chinook that could go into the forties. We'd lose our ability to get our lumber to our cabin sites!

Joel and I hurried to get everything across the swamp before a big melt. We worked all night hauling lumber and plywood before it dawned on us that the temperature was going up because of the

29

heat escaping through the window, not a change in the weather. Mr. Murphy got a couple cheechakos one more time.

Joel built a small cabin. He made himself a table and chair with a hand-macramed seat and back from the lumber of a cottonwood tree he cut down. In the center of the room was a birch pole to provide more roof support. In the middle of the winter it sprouted leaves. There were lots of ribald comments about his dog watering that tree. Very early he started planning his log house he would build one day; one with a lot more space.

Ray was going to live in an old boxcar retired by the railroad that had come in by barge. It got moved around by a bulldozer. Before the winter was over, Ray left the area and gave up the eighty acres he had filed on. Baldy took over that eighty acres to bring his filing up to the one hundred-sixty acres allowed by the BLM.

Baldy had the largest cabin, sixteen by twenty-four feet, so it was the center of life. We played cards, read and gave each other a bad time in the evening. One evening Joel, Ray, and I were playing pinochle. Baldy was reading a book. Suddenly, without saying a word, Baldy put down the book and went to the door. He didn't open the door, but he drew a little black dot on it with a pencil. He picked up his pistol, came over and, laying it on the table, said, "Who can hit the mark on the door?"

The three of us looked at each other with "Now what's this idiot doing?" looks on our faces. Finally I said, "What the hell, it's his door." I picked up the pistol, Baldy moved out of the way, and I aimed at the door. I chickened out. I couldn't pull the trigger in the house.

Baldy asked, "Want me to make the mark bigger?"

"Screw you, Baldy!" I picked up the pistol again and shot the damned dot out. Baldy went over and made a big show of making sure the whole mark was gone.

Then he turned to face the table and asked, "Where is your Jeep parked?" The damned thing was right in front of the door. Needless to say, we all trooped out to check the Jeep. The cabin was on blocks and just high enough that the bullet had gone over the top.

Another day, during a snowstorm, I was at Baldy's alone. I picked up my rifle and started for our place. I walked out the cabin door and spotted a lynx. It was snowing so hard that I could barely see him, and wasn't sure, at first, that I was really seeing a lynx. He finally moved just enough to convince me. In those days, a lynx pelt was worth about forty dollars. I debated a moment, decided I could shoot him without tearing up the hide, and took my shot. That cat simply disappeared. I went over to where he'd been standing. I couldn't see any sign of him; no blood, no nothing. I was almost back to wondering if I'd really seen anything. Maybe the snow and my eyes had ganged up on me.

There were young, very dense spruce trees on three sides of me. I scanned them very carefully, at the bottoms as well as up in the branches. After all, if I had shot a lynx and he wasn't dead, he was probably very upset with me. I walked a small circle around the area and couldn't find any sign. I went back to the spot where the lynx had been. Two or three minutes had passed since my shot. I was standing there, looking down and suddenly became aware that I was looking at a cat's foot. There really had been a lynx and my first reaction was that I had shot its foot off. I reached down to pick it up. I pulled, and the whole damned cat came out of the snow right at me! Thinking it was still alive, I threw that cat about twenty feet! It only took a moment for my breathing to come back to normal and I went over and picked him up again. The bullet had passed clear through him without expanding at all. He'd died instantly and now I had a forty-dollar hide. I brought the animal inside and set it on its stomach with its feet pulled in and propped up its head with a stick so that when someone else came though the door, there was a lynx crouching on the floor. It occurred to me that if I wasn't there, Baldy would shoot the pelt full of holes to turn the joke back on me. So I skinned the cat out.

Baldy, Joel, another guy who was visiting Baldy, and I were across the inlet from Anchorage and needed to get into town. We got up before daylight and went down to the boat. The wind was really blowing the trees around, and we were discussing how rough the water might be. We only had to go five miles to get to Anchorage. None of us gave any thought to the fact that it was early November. The boat was an open dory, twenty-two feet long with a small frame at the bow that had a tarp stretched over the frame so one could store things out of the weather.

We waited for it to get light enough to get a feeling for how rough the water was. It was pretty bad. There was a rip where two currents came together close in, but we figured out a course that would take us through that in fairly short order and then we'd have two to three-foot waves that would be hitting us on the port side for about four and a half miles of travel. Not the most comfortable, but we'd done it before. "Let's do it."

We jumped into the boat and started out. The visitor got in first and crawled in under the tarp to stay dry. We made it through the rip without any problems. Then we got into that beam sea, water moving ninety degrees to us. We were taking spray clear across the boat. Joel, Baldy, and I were soaked in nothing flat. But the damned spray was freezing to the boat. We were gaining weight and losing freeboard like crazy. Joel started bailing the water that was accumulating in the bottom from the spray. He was using a five-gallon bucket and losing ground. I started using my hat because that's all there was that I could use. When you move fast enough, you can bail a lot of water with a hat. Baldy was running the boat and doing a damned good job of making progress, but the boat kept getting heavier and going slower. Ice was about eight inches thick on the upwind side and six inches on the downwind side of the boat.

We pulled into the creek on the Anchorage side with about four inches of freeboard left. We'd lost about sixteen inches of freeboard in less than five miles. A little bit of the last wave climbed in with us, but by then we knew we had it made so we quit bailing. Roy's guest had stayed under the tarp all the time the rest of us were busting our butts trying to stay alive. We got the boat beached and finished bailing the boat so the water wouldn't freeze in it, and said a little prayer that the sun would melt the ice off the sides.

We walked up to my car and our "guest" went to the right front door so he could have the heater. This was too much for me. I doubled up my fists and stuck my nose in his face. "You can ride in the back, or you can walk. Frankly, I'd just as soon beat the snot out of you and leave you here." He opted for the backseat.

Ten years later I was standing on the city dock with a guy from Florida who was working for me. He asked me if all the stories he'd heard about how dangerous the inlet could be were true.

"What have you heard?" I asked.

"Well, I've heard that the water can get really, really rough and that, if you go in the water, the water temperature will kill you in about ten minutes."

So I told him this story. He asked, "Weren't you scared?"

"No, not really. We were either going to make it or we weren't." He looked at me to see if I was putting him on.

"You Alaskans are crazy!"

We came back and forth across Knik Arm long after the few months of the year that the insurance company would insure the boat. They would write coverage from the first of May through the end of September. The rest of the time, because of ice, storms, and other problems, they considered the inlet too dangerous for boating and they were probably correct. We had to make our trip by day as there were no lights, and we had to see to dodge ice that was starting to form on the arm. On one such trip in early

33

November, I came across dressed for the cold and looking like a scruffy bum. That evening I was dressed to take my wife to the opera. Life was varied.

I came home on December 20, 1957. The baby, Jim, was born on December 28. Rita went back to work and I went back across the inlet in late January.

Ice makes for treacherous winter crossings—looking west from Anchorage

Looking east from Point McKenzie towards city of Anchorage

Sometimes the trail got a little rough. These pictures show why swamps were corduroyed and trees were pulled down to stay on high ground when possible.

Standing in the mudhole!

35

Even modern jeeps have a tough go of it over the swampy trail that has had decades of pioneer road work performed on it.

Making repairs 80 miles from the nearest mechanic shop requires a homesteader's field-expedient skills.

CHAPTER 7

JACK

Back in territorial days, it was often said that most development in Alaska was done by men who were too ignorant to realize what they were trying to do wouldn't work. Their methodology was always as unique as their personality and the circumstances dictated. Two of these people were Jack Hart and Don Gezzie, who owned a trucking company based in Anchorage. They decided to go into competition with the Alaska Railroad. They bought an old wooden barge that was actually a ship designed to tow behind a liberty ship during WW II. They brought it and two D-9 cats (Caterpillar tractors or bulldozers) to Anchorage. In 1957, D-9s were the biggest bulldozers made. In those days, and even now to us old-timers, bulldozers of any size or make were called "cats" because the first ones were made by Caterpillar. Jack and Don had decided that they'd create a dock by sinking the barge on the beach at Point MacKenzie and use the two cats to pioneer a cat trail through the Interior. They were going to use "cat trains" to deliver freight throughout Alaska. Believe it or not, this system of delivery had been used for years in the far north and west of Alaska. A cat train consisted of any number of cats pulling a sled big enough to carry a boxcar. Cat trains were very competitive in the far North. To begin with, you can buy a lot of cats for what one locomotive costs. You don't have the expense of laying tracks, either.

We had gotten Joel's cabin built during the winter. It was twelve-by-sixteen feet and was one open room. There was a kitchen area with a small, wood-burning cookstove. There was also a counter area with shelves below for storage. Wall cabinets would come later. The center of the room contained a barrel stove for heat and a table with three chairs. The wall opposite the kitchen area had a set of metal bunk beds. I was staying with Joel when I could be away from Anchorage and doing what I could to build a clearing for our cabin, which we'd start in the spring.

One day Joel and I walked to the "dock site" to see how they were coming. The work crew had most of the ground work done, but didn't have anybody who could run the surveying instruments that controlled setting the barge where it had to be. Joel and I looked at each other and said, "Fellas, this is your lucky day. We just happen to know how to run those instruments." So we went to work.

The crew got the dock set and punched a trail through as far as the Susitna River, about forty miles away. One of the cats broke through the ice at that point. The insurance company decided not to insure any more equipment crossing that river on the ice, and another endeavor bit the dust. The cat became a permanent reef in the river, never to be seen again by the likes of man. I'm not even sure the fish can see it. The river's really muddy right there. We still refer to that trail as the Freight Lines Road and many use it as a way into the cabin. It runs through our land close to the section line.

In payment for the work Joel and I did, we both got fed for two or three days. When one is living with no store nearby, no refrigeration, no running water, a wood cookstove, little money and no one else to do the cooking and cleaning up afterward, being fed good meals was good pay.

After Joel and I had helped place the barge, I got to borrow one of the D-9s for a day. We walked it back to our homestead. I cleared an acre or so of land and leveled the cabin site on the crown of a low hill overlooking a swamp of about one hundred acres. Then I picked exactly where I wanted the cabin to be and dug a trench with the dozer. I planned to span the trench with the cabin. I figured that, once the building was up, I could frame in the space under the cabin and backfill the front and back, thus creating a basement. I got more work done in four or five hours with that dozer than I could have done by hand if I had been able to stay there and work every day through the winter. We also got below the frozen ground while leveling the building site. The next day I was able to lay out the cabin footprint, prove it square by pulling the diagonals, and get in the pilasters that the cabin would sit on. Getting the foundation in gave me a chance to steal a big jump on my construction time.

Our cabin site allowed us to see across the swamp to where Baldy and his dad had homesteaded. There was a ring of primarily white birch trees around our clearing to block the wind and provide summer shade. The trees provided birds and let animals get up closer. Inside the ring was a berm of knocked-down trees that would provide a source of firewood. We'd also have access to the winter sun. I planned, and later built, a cabin with a shed roof sloping south with some fairly large windows in the south wall. This would utilize the sun for light and some warmth during clear days. Our "solar heat" plan worked so well that a number of times that first winter, we let the fire go out in the barrel stove. One of the things we both had trouble getting used to about winters in the North was that the more beautiful and sunny the day, the colder the temperature. The sun would heat the inside of our cabin to eighty to eighty-five degrees, but the outside temperature might be zero or slightly below. As soon as the sun neared the horizon in the afternoon, we'd quickly learn of our mistake of not feeding the stove. Getting the fire going strong enough to prevent losing the sun's heat and keep the cabin from getting really, really cold became a matter of primary importance. While I had the cat, I also got to further develop the trails a little bit by filling in some of the holes we'd created by pulling over trees. We'd had no way to backfill the holes left by the root balls. The D-9 took care of some of that.

I knew one item that would have a large bearing on proving our residency would be the trash pit. I had to get a good one in before freeze up. Rita was in town with Mike and Jim. I was at our cabin with Butch. He and I were doing our best to get the cabin ready for us to live there. He was only five, but he did a great job of handing me tools as I needed them. I selected a spot for the trash pit and started digging. The surface soil at our place was great for digging. It was sandy loam that would hold an almost vertical bank and was easy to dig. It took about two hours to have a pit three-by-four feet and over my head. Butch asked, "How are you going to get out, Daddy?"

"I'm going to dig steps into this corner." Now I find out that if it was easy digging, it probably wouldn't hold my weight as I try to climb out.

"Butch, you're going to have to drag the ladder down here and lower it to me."

He went to the ladder leaning against the cabin. He figured out how to push it over without squashing himself and dragged it to the pit. The tough part was getting one end high enough to get it over the cast pile. I'd thrown dirt up on each side.

"Butch, get in front of the ladder and lift and pull. That way you're only lifting part of the weight." He finally worked it up until he was standing on top of the cast pile.

"Run up to the cabin and bring back the rope hanging on the nail." When he came back, I didn't even have to tell him what to do. He ran one end of the rope though the first ladder rung, pulled until he had two ends even, and threw both ends to me. I tied them to the shovel so I could raise the shovel and pull without pulling the ladder into the cast pile. When I was ready, Butch went to the back end and started pushing. The ladder tipped into the hole. A moment later, I was out of the pit and pulling the ladder up.

RITA

We had three neighbors who played an important role in our homesteading life. Joel was about six years older than Jack and me. He was a bachelor, good looking with dark hair and a beard, and well dressed. He worked as a surveyor and that is where Jack met him. He had no family in Alaska and Jack has always offered friendship, so Joel became part of our life. He filed upon the land next to ours and was there unless he was working in the Bush.

As far as the boys were concerned, Joel was the authority on anything and everything. One day the family was having lima beans for dinner. Mike, our three-year-old, insisted that the beans were English peas. I insisted they were lima beans. After a while Mike decided he would walk over to ask Joel, about a half mile away, if the beans were English peas. He put on his coat and boots and walked outside. It was dark. He stood outside next to the house for maybe ten minutes. Inside, you could hear him brushing up against the house. He came back inside and announced, "He said that they were too English peas."

Roy (Baldy) was one of those people hard to describe, certainly an individual. Jack often remarks that some day he is going to write a book entitled "Alaskan Characters, Two Legged and Four." Baldy would take at least two chapters. He was a few years younger than Jack and about the same size. He also wore a beard. Sometime between the initial filing and year two, Roy married a gal with three kids. Now there was a woman close by for me to visit and kids my kids could play with once in a while. Roy was definitely a leader, always into improving his life, so he added onto his cabin, raised chickens, got a water source, and bought machines to make getting around easier. He had lived most of his life in Anchorage and knew everyone. Roy's father and stepmother were also homesteading. For a while Demaris, Roy's stepmother, was there alone, other times Ed, Roy's dad, was also present. Ed ran a seed store and knew a great deal about the local horticulture. He also had severe heart problems so he was always taking nitro pills.

The other family was Loren and Marcene, the only farmers in the group. They were older than we were by at least ten years, from a farm background in Missouri, so rural life was something they understood. Loren was a small man about five foot eight and one hundred-forty pounds. Marcene was quite a lady, typical of a Midwest farm wife. They hoped to be able to live off the land and make a permanent home. Loren hauled in a sawmill, piece by piece, to create lumber, got a cow for milk, and planted corn in a raised bed. They were planning on canning vegetables and berries. Their two kids were homeschooled.

JACK

When Rita says Loren hauled in a sawmill, haul is an euphemism. He acquired a mill that was driven by a gasoline engine. He and his twelve-year-old son, Doyle, broke the whole thing down into components they could handle together. They brought it across the inlet in a dory and the bunch of us wrestled the components up above the extreme high-tide mark. Then Loren wrapped the whole thing in tarp and left it there until winter. That winter the two of them sledded the whole caboodle, piece by piece, along the beach, across the tidal marsh, and up the bluff to their home-stead, a distance of about four and one-half miles. Lucky them, back there the bluff was only forty feet high.

Loren and his family spent that first winter living in a little log cabin that was maybe twelve by sixteen that they had built. By spring, Loren had cut and drug in enough spruce trees to create enough lumber for a cabin twenty by twenty-four. It boasted a kitchen, living/dining room, and three bedrooms. The partition between Doyle's room and his sister's was very original. If you were looking at an end section of the wall, it came down partway from the ceiling and then offset into Doyle's room thirty inches, the width of a GI cot. Then it went on down to the floor. Doyle had a GI mattress on the "shelf" for his bed, and his sister had a GI cot in her space. This way they had separate bedrooms and one bunk bed.

RITA

Our cabin, on an acre of cleared land, was a twenty-by-twenty-four-foot wide-open room. It had a shed-type roof that sloped toward the south, the source of the winter sun with two large windows and one small one that took up most of the south wall. We had carried in four ten-by-twelve-foot linoleum rugs to cover the floor over tar paper to add insulation. We were to have a barrel stove for heat, more windows, and finished walls and floors. Someday, in my dreams, I would have burlap drapes on windows finished in a natural wood, with a partition of winter-peeled spruce between the living area and the boys' bedroom.

But when Jack came back to town to go to work, the walls were up but lacked wind bracing. The front wall had a six-foot opening where the door would be because he ran out of siding. The windows weren't in. The inside walls were the back side of the Temlock that was the outside skin. Temlock is an oil-soaked paper about an inch thick. It comes in four-by-eight sheets. Many houses were built with it until people covered it with a siding of some sort. It insulated better than plywood, yet was lighter to carry. We had no outhouse, no insulation, and no porch. The cabin was over the trench dug to be a basement, with a log running across the front and a plank from the log to the door. The cabin needed more piling and a front and back wall to the basement, as well as those walls needed to be backfilled. The side walls needed to be cribbed in to stop erosion. We needed bracing, insulation, and interior walls to divide the space into rooms; in other words, tons of work to do.

We planned to stay on our land for fourteen months to complete our residence requirements. The other choice was seven months a year for three years consecutively. Fourteen months meant one year on reduced income among other considerations. We had to be on by July 22. We planned to move the weekend after school closed in late May, but we weren't ready. So while Jack worked and spent what time he could on the land, I repainted the inside of our house to get it ready for renting. The house wasn't paid for, and we were going to spend a winter at the cabin. The house would have to be heated all winter and there was so much vandalism to empty houses, renting was the only thing to do. Besides, it would free up money for other things, like expenses involved in homesteading.

One of those expenses was a boat. Jack found a beautiful used riverboat. It was fiberglass over teak, twenty-four feet long with natural spruce knees, built for the inlet and the Susitna River. Natural spruce knees are from that portion of a spruce tree where the trunk starts and the roots end. This is a ninety-degree angle and much stronger than two pieces of wood nailed together or one piece cut to make a ninety-degree angle. The knee is an important part of the rib that joins the bottom and the side of a boat. Now we could come and go as we needed without counting on others for basic transportation.

School wasn't out yet, but it was spring. Jack and I went over to the cabin, my first trip. Everything was green. The spruce was a dark, almost black shade of green. The birch, willow, and cottonwood were all lighter and different from one another. The fiddlehead fern was still another shade. There were low bush and highbush cranberries, wild roses, lupine, and iris, as well as Labrador tea and the wild hay. There must have been over a thousand shades of green in the Bush that time of year. We landed at the beach and knew we had a given amount of time to make the trip in and back. We started out walking on the trail Jack had built during the winter. I had my parka on. I was carrying the camp stove and a roll of insulation. Jack must have had a rifle, but I don't remember what else. We walked the two and a half miles, but I thought it had to be at least ten. We had not brought along mosquito repellent because we didn't need it in town and I didn't know better. Anyhow, with the stuff I was carrying, I could only swat part of the mosquitoes. The next day I got up and the backs of both my hands were swollen and my forehead was a solid bump. I itched for days, but that amount of venom created an immunity that took years to wear off. The house was all ready by the twentieth of June; the house, but not the Stouts. So on June 30, we rented the house out from under ourselves. We had to move.

Dave said we could live in his cabin because ours wasn't finished. His cabin, an eight-by-twelve one-room affair, up on pilings ten feet or so high, was at the foot of a bluff, or cliff, about ninety feet high. It was furnished with a stove, bed, table and chairs. Dave had built his cabin adjacent to the mouth of a cut in the bluff created by spring runoff of snow melt. This erosion had also created a slough from the beach out about halfway to the low-tide line. Several people beached their boats at the sloughs because they had a little more tide time. This area of Alaska has radical tides. In six hours it can go from thirty-two feet above mean sea level to five feet below. There is little sand on the beach; most of it is clay or mud. Walking through it is a pain in the neck. It is similar to quicksand.

Looking across the swamp to Baldy's cabin on trail into our place

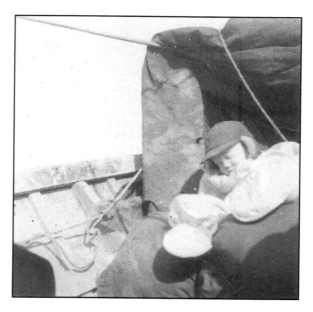

Jim is about eight months old. Blanket sleepers were handy for keeping the baby warm when crossing the inlet.

Our boat was flat-bottomed and constructed entirely of teak with natural spruce knees. It was designed for Cook Inlet and the Susitna River and was a very serviceable boat.

A crossing—Jack, Mike, Butch, and the Armstrongs getting ready to make a trip into Anchorage.

Jack at tiller—1958

CHAPTER 8

RITA

On June 30, 1958, the day Congress passed the Alaska Statehood Bill, we loaded the last of the goods into the boat—we had been moving a little each evening for a week—and sailed into the west. Our neighbor, Sammy, came over from across the street to wish us good luck. Their homestead was up by the Knik River. She brought over two cocktails made of Everclear (190-proof alcohol) and the syrup from fruit cocktail. Those drinks tasted great and hit like a ton of bricks. We were to use their truck to take the last load to the boat. I understood we were to leave the truck at the dock and Carl, her husband, would get it the next day. Jack understood differently. He wanted to take the truck back to Carl and get our car. Jack didn't think he would have time the next day to get the truck returned and he didn't want to inconvenience Carl. As we went through Anchorage to the dock, we were hampered and delayed by twenty to thirty thousand people celebrating statehood. This thronging multitude made the trip take a lot more time so when we finally got to the boat, after three trips through the crowd, our prop was stuck in the mud. We cracked the transom of the boat getting the motor's prop loose. We went out as far as the mouth of the creek. I got out of the boat onto a sand bar standing in the water up to my waist. I was scared but we had to get the motor off the broken side of the transom and onto the other side. Once the motor was on the other side of the transom, we were able to get out of Ship Creek and had an uneventful voyage across the inlet to Point MacKenzie.

Of course we arrived too late to get on the beach, so Jack landed in the mud. After getting the family to the beach, he went back to the boat for the things we needed that night. He brought the food for dinner and milk for the baby, but forgot the baby's bottle. That naturally wasn't discovered until Jack had his clothes off and was in bed. People, that was a night!

48

Oh yes, after fighting our way past thousands of people to get out of town, our reception committee was one little ol' porcupine, a practical example of the extremes of Alaska all in four and a half miles. We could actually hear the people in Anchorage cheering and singing and see the smoke from a huge bonfire while we watched the porcupine wander off along the beach.

Little sleep was had that night. Excitement ran high. Also, the boat had to be moved up or Jack wouldn't get to work the next day. The tide was louder than thunder and at about two thirty in the morning, Jim decided he wanted that bottle! He was tired enough to go to sleep earlier, but not now. So rocking didn't work, nor walking, nor milk in a cup. I finally remembered my mother mentioning an old home remedy. I put a teaspoon of sugar in the corner of a tea towel and tied the towel around the sugar with a piece of string. It made a nipple of sorts that Jim could suck upon. Jim went back to sleep with a sugar tit.

Jack got up and went out and fixed the anchor so the boat would float up to shore. About five in the morning, the family got up and dressed. Jack and I ate and went out to unload before he went back across the inlet to work. I was walking in my bare feet because I couldn't find boots to fit and didn't want to get my shoes covered with mud. That clay is slippery in bare feet, so walking was like a dance upon ice. I had on light-blue pants that I pulled off to keep them clean. Jack kept making remarks about my bare bottom as we pushed the boat off.

The next week was a very uneventful time. Jack worked in town and came home at night. The kids and I rested. The beach was clean and sunny all day. We had picnic suppers because we could gather driftwood, build a campfire, and bake potatoes. We timed it so just as the potatoes were done the tide would put out the fire. The boys went wading when the water at last got to sand. The water was so filled with glacier silt that if they went in as deep as their ankles they could not see their toes. Besides, it was cold. During the day I helped them build sand castles.

CHAPTER 9

RITA

Bears were everywhere. There had never been so many people around before, so the bears were not the least bit bashful. One day during lunchtime, a bear came into the area and stole the kids' teddy bears from under the cabin. I have no idea what the bear thought he had, but when he got tired of his game, he left the toys up in an alder bush growing up on the bluff along the trail. The kids wanted their dad to help them find the toys. Michael's "Big Monkey" was a prized possession and Butch got the teddy bear when he was six weeks old. Daddy kept putting them off, saying he would when he had time. When Dad spotted the toys in the kids' hands, he questioned both boys.

JACK

"I thought you said the bear took those toys from under the cabin."

"We did."

"Then how come you have the bear and monkey in your hands now?"

"Well, Daddy, you were so busy we decided to do the job ourselves."

"You did what?"

"We took a rifle and tracked the bear up the trail and into that bunch of alder. Then Mike climbed the bush and I stood guard 'til he had thrown the toys down. Then we hightailed it back to the cabin before Mother missed us."

"But you didn't have a rifle."

"Oh, yes, we did," they both claimed. "See, here it is." Butch held up a toy rake from a kid's gardening set. After that, the stuffed toys went to bed with the kids.

RITA

Dave needed his cabin for the fishing season, so Jack and I borrowed another cabin, Roy's. Jack and I carried everything back using the Jeep as far as possible, but there was a big mud puddle across the trail. Every time a machine went through it, the puddle grew in all directions. We tried to avoid making it permanent by walking the last part of the trip. We carried the baby and things that had to be carried, but had Mike and Butch walk, except for the puddle. Jack had Mike on his shoulders and Butch in his arms when Jack slipped. Mike lost his balance and Jack caught Mike's foot under his arm. So he walked through the mud, one kid in his arms, another by the foot under his armpit. Mike was dangling upside down. All the way across the puddle Mike kept saying, "Don't slip again, Daddy!" Mike was glad to walk the rest of the way.

This second cabin was much bigger: sixteen by twenty-four. It was about half a mile back into the woods. This was the cabin where the guys had headquartered all last winter. It was furnished and had an apartment-size propane stove. There was no plumbing. This meant that all water had to be hauled outside to be dumped. I washed the dishes after lunch one day, carried the pan over to the door, and set it on the barrel stove to open the bar latch on the door. I turned and picked up the pan and then turned to go through the door, except the door was occupied. A large black bear was there watching the door to see what was causing the noise he could hear coming from inside. I did the only thing I could do. I threw the water at the bear in the doorway. He sat down to brush the soapy water out of his eyes as I used my foot to close the door.

Bears, like most wild animals, tend to have a population cycle. This was a summer when the bear population was high. One night we were in bed on the floor. The kids were asleep. We were enjoying a little grown-up time together. I looked up to see a bear looking at us through the window. Talk about coitus interruptus. I don't know who was the most startled, us or the bear.

I watched one bear come into the clearing while the boys were eating lunch. The bear butted the soccer ball around just like the dog had. He opened his mouth and bit down. He punctured the hard rubber ball with his teeth. I surely didn't want one to bite any part of me. One of our neighbors had a bear come into the tent while they were eating lunch and the bear took the hotdogs off the table. I know why the people let the bear have their meal.

On Saturday of the first week, Jack went off to "corduroy" the swamp. The narrowest point was about one hundred yards. To build a "corduroy," he was cutting spruce trees to place close together to form a path across the tundra. This path would spread out the weight of the Jeep and let one travel across. He came back for lunch and the whole family returned with him. The baby was in a sleeping bag in the back of the Jeep covered with Off, a spray insect repellent, to protect him from mosquitoes. Jack and I got a little done while Mike, our three-year-old sang. He would take the words of a song and change them to his vocabulary. The results were amazing. This day he was singing, "She was peaches, she was honey, and she cost me all my daddy's dollars."

After corduroying about fifty feet, we decided to see if we could drive the rest of the way. We all got into the Jeep and, with a silent prayer, we started. A wet ride was had by all, but we made it to the other side. The kids stood up in back, hanging onto the roll bar. I braced my feet and held on with one hand while holding the baby with the other. Back to our own cabin we went. It was beautiful to us alone. I laid the linoleum and Jack checked everything. All too soon it was time to return. We still had a door to hang, but first we had to finish the wall.

CHAPTER 10

RITA

We returned to town Sunday night. I wanted to do the laundry Monday morning, so we rented a motel room for the night. Of course, Jim cried like never before. Jack had to be at work early in the morning, so I took Jim and went for a ride. I decided to go by the house and check the mail. I got the mail from the mailbox near the road. No one was there. Sammy, the gal that lived across the street, was up so I went over to see if she could help me fix Jim's bottle, as the milk wouldn't come out. Sammy was able to fix the bottle and told me that no one had been near our house. She also told me that Phyllis, a neighbor from when we lived in Bootleggers Cove, had a message about my nephew arriving. I went on back to the motel.

The next day I went to see Phyllis. She said my sister, Dorothy, had called from Los Angeles. Dot had sent a telegram that had been returned and had tried to call us, and Jack's folks but had been unable to reach anyone. So, in looking through old letters trying for a phone number, she had come across Phyllis's Christmas card and had called her. Phyllis had tried to reach us but, of course, couldn't. Many people that Phyllis did contact told her how—in one way or another—she might reach us, but she kept on trying 'til she had half of Anchorage looking for us. I learned from my visit with Phyllis that my nephew Robin was to arrive Tuesday at noon. I sent a telegram that I would meet him.

Sixteen-year-old Robin was to stay until his school started in September. We had invited him in May and never got a response from him or his mother, so we had forgotten all about it. He was invited because we knew we would need help and he could and would give it, and at the same time have a very different summer vacation. We also found out that the people who had been so eager for our house didn't want it, so we had to rent it again.

I called the paper and placed an ad. Robin and I cleaned up the mess the non-renters had made and waxed the floors. The day after the ad was in the paper, we rented the house again.

Finally, after a hectic week in town and the workday done, we returned to Baldy's cabin where we were temporarily staying. Things had changed somewhat while we were gone. A bear had broken in. One would have thought he had a grudge against us. What a mess! What a greeting for weary travelers coming home. There was approximately forty dollars worth of food all over the floor: flour, sugar, beans, noodles, canned food, powdered milk, and canned milk. All of this was just inside the door in front of the shelves. Forty dollars bought a lot of food in 1959, eight or nine grocery bags full. One bed had two great big piles of dung right in the center. The bear had stood up and urinated all over the stove. He had bitten into a can of mosquito dope and gotten sick all over the floor. Over all was the sickening stench of bear. Boy, they do stink. Robin, Jack, and I manned the broom, shovel, and various buckets, and in an hour and a half you could move around the house. We put a sheet over the broken window to keep out the bugs and went to bed. Jack had to go back to town in the morning for work.

What a bear can do to your cabin—late 1980s break-in

BEFORE BEAR

Late 1980s—nice and neat cabin interior

After Bear

What a bear can do to your cabin—late 1980s break-in

"Well, what can you do?"

After Bear

This bear came in through the front door—late 1980s break in

Late 1980s bear damage, and they eat foam rubber!

The day before, when we had gotten to the beach, we had too much to pack in, so we stacked some stuff under Dave's cabin. About eleven o'clock I sent Robin down to Dave's cabin to bring back a box of food. Robin was born and reared in Los Angeles, California. He was a fine, strapping boy and a lot of help. His only drawback was being totally deaf, sometimes making it hard to communicate, although he read lips very well. He also ate so much we had to make one extra trip to town each week to keep enough food for him. Between feeding Robin and Jack teaching him to shoot, he was pretty expensive labor. However, we were all very fond of Robin. The kids worshiped him and Butch ran his five-year-old legs into the ground to go everyplace with him and, if it were possible, we would have kept him for the winter.

Robin was at the beach, and I was outside with the three boys. Suddenly I looked to the edge of the clearing and there sat a large black male bruin. To say I was totally startled would have been an understatement. That darn bear wasn't over fifty feet away, just sitting there like a big dog, an awfully big dog. While I watched, he picked up some bacon he had evidently dropped the day before and started eating it. I tried to scare him away by banging on a dishpan. This had worked on another occasion. That darn fool didn't even know he was supposed to be frightened. He just cocked his head to one side as though waiting to see if the next act would be as entertaining. While I stood looking at the bear and he at me, and trying to think of something else to scare him away, Robin came into the clearing. He had a box of groceries on his shoulder and was watching the ground. Finally he looked up and it didn't take too much brainpower to realize I was acting a little strange, even for me. After deciding something was amiss, he looked around for a reason and his eyes fell upon the bear. Robin put the box down on a gas drum near the chopping block, picked up the ax, and started over to me. At this point the bear decided that either the cast or the show stank and he departed. I decided that instead of going back for more at the beach, Robin had better stick around. This, I was to learn, was a big mistake.

We had about a half-hour intermission, and then our furry audience came back into the clearing. We again tried noise to drive him away. No luck. So we all went into the cabin. Now we had a sheet between us and the bear. There we watched through another window, as the bear worked his way around the clearing. He had food cached all around on trails to the garbage pit. Of course, in the pit was all the residue from his feast of the day before. It seemed to me that there should have been enough for a two-day orgy. It would have fed us for a month. The damned bear gorged himself for an hour and a half or so when another bear came into view. Bruin number two spent several minutes trying to work an invitation to the party. All he got for his effort was a good roughing up. Bear number two was a skinny, hungry-looking thing and probably needed a good square meal.

After whipping the other bear and running him off to the other side of the clearing, bear number one decided he'd had enough of the garbage pit and would try elsewhere. There were only two other places apparent in the immediate vicinity. One was a five-gallon garbage can right outside our sheet-covered window, and the other was inside the cabin. Right then I decided to break out the fire power. I went to the gun rack, and then I realized my mistake. Two days before, Dave had borrowed our 30.06, a beautiful handmade rifle that is the pride of my husband's heart. I could have sent Robin for that rifle when we first came in, but now it was too late. That left us with plenty of ammo for the 30.06 and for our .270, but that rifle was sixty-five miles away at Jack's folks. We also had two .22s, but no shells, and a twelve-gauge shotgun with lots of trap shot, a few birdshot, and two slugs. What a mess. I didn't know what to do. I was just learning to shoot and when I hit anything it was luck.

Robin was not a great deal better. He had been raised without a father in a city by city people. The only man in his life was his Uncle Joe, who neither owned nor wanted a gun. While I stood there going crazy, Robin decided to act. He took down the shotgun, took the two slugs and six shells, and loaded up. He and Jet, our toy cocker, went out to do battle with the bears. Jet immediately chased the skinny one off, while Robin yelled and waved at the more belligerent one. He still wouldn't bluff. Jet came back and rushed the other bear. Wham! The bear got him with a left hook to the face. Jet ran back to the door and we grabbed him. At this point, the bear made his intentions known by coming right on toward us.

The bear was only walking toward us, as though to see if we would back off, so Robin let him walk up to about thirty feet and then Robin fired. Robin got him right in the face. The only trouble was Robin had loaded the bird shot last, so it came up first. Instead of splitting the bear's skull, he only perforated his hide. The bear stopped and pawed at his face. While he was doing that, Robin tried to work another shell into the chamber. He succeeded in jamming the gun.

The bear didn't know the gun was jammed, but he didn't like what he had just found out about guns, so Robin and I stood and watched while the bear ran off. Now we had a wounded, probably damned mad, bear in the woods. We again retired to the cabin. We were rid of the bear for the moment, but now I had real worries. In the first place, there was a wounded bear near the cabin, and in the second place, my husband had given me strict orders not to shoot the bears. Never occurred to me that I had spent the day in a bear cache, a very dangerous place to be.

JACK

What a grand finale for a day. Here I come walking into the clearing around the cabin, full of love, happy to be home, and eager to see my family. I shouted, "Hello, the cabin!" The door opened. Everyone came charging out. Everybody was shouting at once. Thinks I, what a beautiful welcome. My heart filled with joy. My happiness knew no bounds. Then, as they near, the words of my number one son penetrated and shattered my bubble of bliss. "Daddy, Daddy, Robin shot a bear. He shot him in the face and he ran off that way." Oh woe, my world is shattered. I am desolate. Not only has my wife done exactly what I have asked her not to do, but just what I feared has come to pass. There is a wounded bear for me to track and kill.

But I am a man of forbearance. I will listen to my wife's tale before I explode and show my wrath. She quieted the kids and began her tale. As I listened, the clouds of woe were dissipated, the sun shone again. They had been brave. They tried to do as I say, but the bear gave them no choice. In a moment of crisis, they acted bravely and well. What matter Robin loaded the gun wrong. His spirit was strong. To go up against two bears with two slugs, and for Rita to go out to back him up with no gun, but with a great fear of bears, was a magnificence that would make any man's heart fill with pride. What matter I had to walk all the way back to the beach for a rifle, what matter I was tired. What matter I had to track a wounded bear. Now my heart was full of pride in my family as well as love. My cup was full, even if my stomach was empty.

Anyway. Robin and I went to the beach and got the .06. When we got back, Robin showed me where the bear had entered the woods, looking around to help me locate the blood trail, if any. There was blood on some leaves, and it didn't take me long to realize Robin's eyes were a great deal sharper than mine. So I says, says I, "Robin, if you wish to go with me, I will teach you what I know about tracking." Without anything but a desire to learn and a trust in my rifle eye, Robin set out with me. I showed him what I knew as we went along and, just as in most everything else, Robin picked it up immediately. After about a half hour of slow work, I heard a slight noise off to the left. I motioned to Robin to stay put on the trail while I went to investigate. I knew if we both left the trail, we would lose it. The noise I heard turned out to be the bear. He had become aware that we were behind him and circled back on his own trail. He was sitting in a small depression in the swamp waiting to nail us. If we'd stayed on his trail he'd have had us in the swamp also, and the bear would have heard every move we made. When we got up beside him, he'd have hit us at about forty miles an hour. A man's got to be damned good and damned lucky to handle that. As it was, I'd been lucky enough to hear one noise he made and by cutting across the circle he'd taken, was able to spot him just before entering the swamp. The bear had either heard or smelled me. When I spotted him, he had his nose in the air trying to place me by smell. The movement of raising my rifle must have caught his eye, because he saw me just as I pulled the trigger. The bullet moved faster than he could. The bear dropped so fast he fell below my barrel and was completely out of sight before I lowered my rifle. I hadn't realized until then that I had closed my left eye. Well, now I had to walk up on a bear I had just shot but couldn't see. I was sure he was dead because I had shot at his head.

I moved to where I could see Robin and called him ahead. We waited a few minutes to see if the bear would move. No movement, so I told Robin to stay put, took the dog that had arrived after the shot, and moved on in. The bear was dead. Jet landed on him with all four feet and grabbed a mouthful of fur. He was getting even with that bear. I touched Jet on the butt with the rifle barrel when I walked up. That dog went three feet into the air and tried to go four ways at once.

Robin went back to the cabin and got a piece of one-inch pipe and some rope. When we had staggered through the swamp and gotten the bear up by the cabin, the pipe was bent in the middle. That damn bear must have weighed 450-500 pounds. We took pictures of Robin posing by the bear and then dressed it out. He wasn't real good eating, but we ate quite a bit and gave the rest away. We would take the skull into town to the Fish and Wildlife. They gather data on animals and in return, you get your skull back all nice and clean. After it was clean, Robin could take it back to California with him.

Retrospect makes it obvious that we were luckier than we deserved in relation to the bear. Our naivete was amazing, even if it was our first major encounter with a bear. As Rita mentioned, I had loaned the .06 rifle to a neighbor because of his trouble with a bear. I should have gone and gotten it while Rita started cleaning the cabin. I didn't do that. We should have expected the bear to return and try to reclaim the cabin. We didn't. I should have loaded the shotgun and shown Robin how to use it. I didn't. Had I loaded the shotgun, I'd have loaded it so that a slug would have come up first. Judging by the shot pattern in the bear's face, Robin would probably have missed the bear. A defensive loading of a shotgun usually has a slug first, figuring on a first shot at thirty-five to fifty yards. The second shot is backup for the first and is usually buckshot. My experience has been, in each case, when facing a specific life and death moment for the first time, it's luck that brings you through it. The bear didn't charge; it walked to Robin, expecting to just take him out. The real courage was on Robin's part. It took a lot of courage for a kid one day out of Los Angeles to let that bear walk up until he could be sure of his shot. I don't know many people who could do that.

CHAPTER 11

JACK

This was fast becoming the "long hot summer" and it's a good thing that we had almost twenty-four hours of daylight. It seemed that we needed every one of them. I was working construction in town, commuting each way by boat and splitting my time on Point MacKenzie between our place and Baldy's. We were working ten-hour days on the job. Commuting included shopping, getting to the boat, getting the boat in the water, making the run to the point, setting the boat to catch the next morning's tide, and making my way to the cabin. The time we were at Baldy's wasn't too bad because I only had about a half mile to walk. Once we got back into our place, I had two and a half miles to go each way.

Rita and Robin were great contributors to getting things done. I never did get the swamp corduroyed all the way across. Except for the two days of concentrated effort, it was one of those things we worked on as time permitted. There was almost always something that had higher priority. We'd drive to the edge of the swamp, park the Jeep, load everything on our backs, and walk a mile back to the cabin.

The reason our cabin wasn't quite ready when we first got to the point at the end of June was because there was still a space about six feet wide in one wall that had yet to be filled. Joel, Baldy, Ray, and I started erecting our cabin in early April. We'd gotten the floor, walls, and roof done. When I'd gotten ready to hang the door, I discovered that the wall had racked just enough that the studs weren't plumb enough to hang a door on them. I discovered that fact just at a time when I didn't have time to correct the problem, because I had to catch the tide to get back to town. It's hard to explain how the tide can rule your life if you've never had to live with it. You know the old saying, "Time and tide wait for no man." Well, when the tide differential runs from twenty-seven feet to thirty-eight feet, it's especially domineering. When I got back to town, Rita said, "Someone from M.B. called. The name and phone number are by the phone." I called and found that they'd like me to go to work Monday morning. We started working six tens. That didn't leave me any time to get back and fill the hole in our wall.

Now, in early July, this was the day to fill the hole. We all went back from Baldy's. The first thing we discovered was that a bear had been in to check out my progress, or lack thereof. He hadn't done any real damage because there wasn't any food. He did bite into a can of roofing tar. Based upon tracks and the scattering of tar, it would have been really funny to watch him try to get rid of that can stuck to his teeth. It probably didn't taste very good. Even when he succeeded in letting go of the can, he still had a lot of tar in his mouth. I doubt that bear ever bit another can. Rita and Robin cleaned up the bear's mess using white gas while I got ready to hang the door. First I framed the opening. We covered the hole next to the door with five layers of tarpaper on both sides because we had run out of Temlock. We hung a door Charlie gave us that used to be the door to his girls' bedroom. It was pink on one side and yellow on the other. Very handy for notes like, "shut off propane." We used that door for many years until a bear finally broke through it by leaning on it until the center panel gave way.

RITA

Shortly after Robin arrived, it became apparent that we could not survive if Jack continued to work all week in Anchorage. He was trying to work and commute back and forth across the inlet on a radical tide cycle. He had no place to stay in town, and some nights he had to sleep in the car. Those nights he had no shower to get ready for work the next day. It really boiled down to either he quit working and take care of us on the homestead, or we give up the whole deal and move back to town. I don't think we considered going back to town, but we had to have a place to stay and a road to get about. We may have just given up if I had not had a job for September.

While Robin was with us, Jack and I made a trip to town to do the laundry and shop for food. We got off the boat and Jack lowered the top of his hip boots so he looked like the prince from Puss and Boots. We were walking on Fourth Avenue, the main street in Anchorage. Jack and I both became aware that people were staring at us. I jokingly asked Jack if the back of my pants were split out. Then someone asked if he could take our picture. We looked at each other. Nothing strange to us, two people in jeans and boots. I was wearing a sweatshirt and Jack a work shirt. We did look like somebody who'd just come in from the Bush, but we were relatively clean and couldn't really understand why anyone would want our picture but we said, "Okay." Then we kept on walking among the tourists who were all looking at us like we were the strange ones. We went into the sporting goods store and about that time Jack sneezed. He reached for his handkerchief in his back pocket. It was then that the mystery was solved. Jack had forgotten to take off his pistol when he reached the boat. He wore a .357 revolver tied down to his leg when walking through the woods because, if it wasn't tied down, it constantly worked its way back until it was between the packboard and his hip. He couldn't take a rifle everywhere he went. He needed the gun in case he met an unfriendly bear and had to have his hands free to do any work. Those tourists must really have wondered if they were in the Hollywood version of the Last Frontier. People walking down the main street of the town and wearing a revolver tied down like an old gunslinger was quite a sight. They pay people today to do that in Tombstone and those guns are shooting blanks.

JACK

When we got back to Point MacKenzie, we found our Jeep upside down at the bottom of the cut to the beach. We had been having trouble starting the Jeep, so we would park at the top of the gully. We'd start the Jeep by pushing the clutch in and once it was rolling down the hill, let the clutch out. Someone borrowed the Jeep while we were in town and messed up getting it started. We got it turned over, but couldn't get it started until someone had time to work on it. So we walked.

Nobody owned up to rolling the Jeep. Carrying rifles, Baldy and I walked about a mile west of the gully along the beach. There were five fishermen cabins kind of clustered there. I stood back with the rifle, far enough that my peripheral vision covered the area and Baldy went up and knocked on a door. A guy answered the knock.

Baldy said, "Hi. I'm Baldy and this is Jack. We have a Jeep back down that way. Today someone tried to borrow it and they accidentally rolled it over. We were wondering if you might have seen someone."

"No, I didn't see anybody."

"Okay, thanks a lot." And Baldy went to the next cabin. We figured two were enough. By the time the guys in the cabins had talked out the fact that those crazy homesteaders had come around looking for a gunfight, we wouldn't have to worry about them anymore.

RITA

That winter Jack and Roy tried to take the Jeep down the beach to Goose Bay. They got stuck and before they could get the Jeep out again, the tide came in. Once the tide got to the motor, we had no more hope for transportation.

CHAPTER 12

RITA

We had just been back to our cabin a few days. By then, bears were not cute little things to watch. We knew that they did as they damn well pleased. We got up one morning and in the clearing was a mama and two cubs. The dog ran at the sow, and she put the cubs up a tree and ran off. With her cubs up the tree, we knew she would be back. Jack got his rifle and Robin got his camera. Between the dog and Robin in front of him, Jack had a problem on his hands. If the dog charged and the bear charged back, Jack was going to end up with a dog between his legs and a bear on his chest. So Jack was forced to shoot and kill the sow. Next, the two cubs started crying, "maamaa," and our kids started crying, "Don't you shoot those baby bears!"

Jack decided he could capture the cubs and take them to the Fish and Wildlife, and they would find them a home somewhere other than our front yard. It took a long time to capture those little guys. They were huddled together on a branch of a birch tree about twenty feet up. Jack got a pole eight feet long and fashioned a noose on the end of it. Then he went up the tree after the cubs. The first cub was easy. When Jack stuck the pole out at him, the cub swatted at it and Jack was able to snare the cub's front leg in the noose and pull the loop tight. He swung the cub out so that he couldn't grab either the tree or Jack, and then Jack worked his way down the tree to a point where he could lower the cub enough to allow Robin to get another poled loop around the little guy. Then Jack climbed on down and helped Robin truss up the squirming little bundle of rage and fear so he'd stay put. That wasn't real easy. The guys were trying to be gentle, but the cub was doing his best to make one or both of them bleed. He only weighed about thirty-five pounds, but every pound of him was trying really hard to make Jack and Robin sorry they'd ever met him.

These two little guys cost us a whole day. Jack has one in his arms. Nephew Robin from Los Angeles, staying with us for the summer, is playing with the little guy that was "friendly," at least he didn't try to bite.

That was the end of easy. Jack went up the tree after the second bear. The cub went higher. Robin went up an adjacent tree and got above the cub. The little critter jumped to another tree, went down and ran to another tree and climbed it. This scene repeated itself over and over for at least two hours. Finally, Robin and Jack had the cubs tied up. One tamed down, but the second wanted to bite and scratch. The men loaded the bears onto a sled and pulled the sled to the beach, put the bears into the boat, and took them to town. The cubs were turned over to the Fish and Wildlife so they could be placed where they would survive.

I decided that we must have windows in all walls after that morning. We had big windows on the south side to let in the sun all winter, but the other three sides were solid wall. So, while Jack was busy catching bears, I was busy putting in windows. First I had to decide where. Next I decided how high. When Jack brought in the building supplies, he brought in two windows that were four by two feet and two that were two feet square. I placed one window in the middle of each of the three walls as high as I could to offer protection from bears coming in, and yet we could still see out. The bigger windows went into the north and west sides, with the little one over the kids' bed and the corner of the south wall. The cabin was built with studs twenty-four inches on center. I cut out the center stud for the north window by the door and for the west window. Next I put in a two by four to be the bottom support. A framed-in window has a header, so I attached another two by four above. I know now that the header is supposed to have a stud under each end but mine didn't. All my two by four did was provide a receptacle for the nail to hold the window in. After I got the frame in place, I cut out the Temlock that was the outside skin of the building. When I was in second grade, we built a town out of boxes. To cut out the windows, we drilled a hole in each corner and then cut from hole to hole using a coping saw. I did the same thing now, except I used a keyhole saw. Because the window was too big for the opening, I sawed off the extra part of the window frame with a hand saw. All I had to do now was lift in the window and hold it in place using a couple of nails on each side, inside and out. "Now, let there be light," said I. I could see in every direction. No more opening the door to meet a bear.

About a week after we moved into our cabin, I heard the train whistle blow. It sounded like it was just out of sight down the Freight Lines Road. Remember, I had walked from the beach, waded through the mud, and helped to pack our things to the cabin. When I heard that whistle, I thought the train had to be just over the hill and I was ready to kill my husband for all he had put me through rather than take the train. The Alaska Railroad will stop anywhere, and I could not understand why we had not used it.

I learned that the train was just leaving Anchorage and it didn't come anywhere near us. For some reason, on some days, the noise from Anchorage is carried by the wind to the cabin. We could hear the traffic going up Romig Hill in the winter. We set our clock by the noon whistle that blew every Friday at eleven thirty to test for civilian defense, because we had no other way to check the time while we lived in the cabin. There were other occasions when it was so quiet that one could hear the leaves fall off the trees.

Because we had to carry everything in to the cabin, furniture and fixtures were limited. I had carried in a Coleman camp stove the first time we walked in. White gas came in five-gallon cans. Anyhow, for cooking, I had two burners. Water was carried from a spring at the beach, three miles away, in a five-gallon jerry can. We drank instant coffee so as not to waste water perking coffee or washing the pot. We ate a lot of one-pot meals. I tried rice, mushroom soup, canned green beans, and salmon. I still think it is a good meal. Jack had never liked casseroles, but I couldn't figure out any other way to feed us. We usually had oatmeal with powdered milk for breakfast and we ate a lot of peanut butter sandwiches. Because we had no electricity, we had no refrigeration. Therefore, we had little fresh meat until winter because we couldn't keep meat cold.

JACK

One of the few things we carried in that wasn't truly "have-to-have" was a bag of spice drops. Spice drops are small gumdrops of different flavors. I would turn my back on the room each morning and take a double handful of spice drops from the bag and then turn back to the kids and have them pick a color. Nobody knew how many they were going to get because the number per color always varied. It was a neat little tradition that was family inclusive and had a slight bit of competitive tinge to it because someone was going to get the most candy, based upon the color chosen, and it was different each day. That was about all the sugar we got besides a little on our oatmeal.

RITA

Jack manufactured the barrel stove in town. First he had to find a heavy barrel and a "Yukon stove kit": the door with a draft built in, legs, and a collar to attach the chimney. Using the door for a pattern, he cut out the opening in the end of the barrel and drilled holes to attach the legs. He used a sledgehammer to flatten the top side so we would have a flat surface for pots and kettles. Now all he had to do was get it to the cabin. He used the Jeep to get the barrel to the neck of the swamp that still needed corduroying. The swamp was now too wet to drive across. When Jack got as far as he could with the Jeep, he tied the barrel to his packboard and walked about two steps. He was so loaded he fell over backward. The only solution was to split up his load. He put the things he was leaving inside the stove and shut the door, and the rest he brought into the cabin. When he went back the next day for the stove, it was obvious that a bear had decided to investigate. The door was open, the stuff pulled out, and the barrel was down the bottom of a hill. It was weeks later, on a hunting trip, that Jack found out the bear had bitten the air mattress he had left inside the barrel.

Once we got the barrel stove set up, we used it for heat and for a slow cooker. We could cook things like beans and stew or soup. We used the top of the barrel for melting snow for water and for heating that water. I would put the metal dishpan on the stove, fill it with dirty dishes and snow, and by the time the water was hot, the dishes were clean. Everyone always was expected to clean their plate so that the dishes were easier to do. Between the lack of access to the store, the amount of money we didn't have, no refrigeration, and a limited water supply, we ate simply.

JACK

We ate a heck of a lot of moose meat once the weather got cold enough to keep it cool. I remember one evening when I was helping Rita get dinner on the table. She handed me a plate of moose and said, "Here, cut some meat up for the boys." I cut what I thought was enough for the boys. Rita took it from me and put it all on one plate and handed it back to me to cut some more. Those kids went through three-quarters of a moose in just over three months, and they were still so small they had to have their meat cut for them. Imagine what it was like by the time they became teenagers. In fact, one time when we got rid of two of the boys at the same time, our food bill went down 50 percent. I told Rita, "Let's ship them all out to your mother for a month. The grocery store will owe us money."

Her answer, "It won't work. Besides, they'd give Mom a heart attack."

RITA

Because of the bugs, we needed to keep the door closed. Sometimes it was too hot to be shut in. We covered one window opening with screen. We took out the nails holding the window in so we could open it. Now all we needed were some hinges. We took a leather checkbook cover and cut and folded the cover into two rectangles about one by three inches and nailed them to the window and to the two-by-four framing. Now we could open a window for fresh air. That window also served as an icebox in the winter. A Missouri latch, a two-inch piece of wood loosely nailed so it would turn, kept it closed.

Shortly after Robin left for California, Jack and I were in bed one morning when something hit the house. Jack said, "That was a spruce hen."

I asked him why he didn't go shoot it. It would be fresh meat and we were short of fresh meat. Jack got up and put on his slippers and took his .22 rifle outside and shot two birds. Then he came back inside and put on some clothes and went out to find the birds. The dog did a great job finding the birds in the brush. Jack cleaned the birds and I got the rest of the meal ready. It wasn't the most successful meal I have ever prepared. The birds were tough. They needed to age.

One of our neighbors decided to train his dog to retrieve ducks. He shot a duck and the dog brought it to him. He praised the dog and then tossed the duck as far as he could and told the dog to fetch. Again, the dog did as he was supposed to. Next time the duck was thrown and the dog was ordered to fetch it, the dog picked up the duck and ran off and proceeded to eat it. I guess he decided he would rather play fetch with a ball.

We needed to do the laundry, so Jack and I got up early and started for town. It took all day to get to town, wash the clothes, shop for groceries, and get back to the cabin. One had to make the tide to accomplish everything. We started out that morning with Jack carrying the laundry and Mike. I had Jim on my back. We tied Jim to a packboard that had a metal seat at the bottom with the strings going in an "X" across his chest. He could lean up against my back. He wore a navy watch cap and when the bugs got too bad, he pulled the cap down over his face and went to sleep. Butch walked. When we got to the swamp where Jack had corduroyed, we were able to jump from log to log, getting across and keeping our feet dry. I had on Tuffy boots, high-top leather Red Wing boots made for boys, so I wanted to stay dry. We had a busy day and were walking home before dark. Now Jack had the groceries we had bought and Mike on his back and when we got to the swamp, he carried Butch in his arms. I now had Jim and a duffel bag full of clean clothes on my back.

Jumping from log to log was not so easy now. I got about halfway across when I missed a log. I landed on my rump with the log under my knees. I couldn't stand up because I couldn't lean forward. Jack was ahead of me and had no hands to help me up. He went on across the swamp while I sat in the wet. After putting Mike and Butch down, he came back and helped me to my feet. I got across the rest of the swamp and dripped the rest of the way home.

Our in-town babysitter had given us a couple of hand-me-down swings called Billy Boys. They had a wooden seat about fifteen inches long with a fork up front. A piece of metal shaped like a capital "I" was bolted through the fork at the front of the seat. The top of the capital "I" made a handle and the bottom of the capital "I" made a footrest. The swing system hung by a three-part bridle. One rope went to each side of the handle and the third rope went to the back of the seat. The rider pumped the swing by pushing and pulling on the handle, while doing the reverse on the footrest. Jack tied a trunk of a tree between two other trees for a crossbar and attached the swings to the crossbar. The kids loved those swings. They could really make them fly. One would sit on the seat and the other would stand facing him with his feet on the footrest hanging on to the front ropes. The capital "I" was between the boys. Both would pump. With the two of them pumping, they could get that swing going so high that the ropes would actually go slack. With eyes shining, they would be grinning at each other as they free fell until the ropes became tight. One day a rope broke during a flight and then the boys really did fly.

Fortunately no one was hurt, but they landed ten feet away by the woodpile. I know boys will be boys, but mommies get scared never-the-less.

Three Boys—Late August 1958
John (Butch) is five, Mike is three, and Jim is seven months old.
Joel, our fourth boy, was born two years later, in August 1960.

Laundry Day

Mike was three, therefore he got to ride. The coat kept the bugs off and was needed on the boat for warmth. Note the pistol tied down on Jack's right leg.

Jim and Rita

Jim is tied to a pack board along with life jackets for the boat trip to town to do the laundry. The coat—you either wear it or carry it. The peanut butter and jelly sandwich was breakfast and in the pocket is a clean diaper. The metal walkway was a runway mat used by the military during WW II. Here it is placed on top of logs we used to corduroy the swamp. These pictures were taken about 8 a.m.

CHAPTER 13

RITA

I don't remember how the discussion of a school and a community for the point got started, but it was before we moved to the cabin. Everyone believed that the causeway was going to be built "tomorrow" and that area would become a bedroom community to Anchorage. A school in the area was a way to let people live there in the meantime. I was hired to be the teacher. An enterprising gentleman from Anchorage, Ken Hinchey, was interested in putting in a road from Goose Bay to the point to hook up to the Freight Lines Road. He promised to help get a road from the Stout's cabin to the school site, and this meant that there were quarters for the teacher if I was the teacher. Jack tried very hard to get a road from our place to the school. He went to town in August and called Ken Hinchey and arranged to fly over and look for a road south. He flew over about 4 p.m. and buzzed the house. That is about as close to a road as we ever got. The plan was that Jack was going to drive me back and forth and babysit our kids. It would be tough, but it could work. It would provide money for us to live on and that was very important. It was twelve miles away and Jack figured the road could all be high ground. In the beginning everyone was going to help, but as time went on everyone decided that it was only important to us; therefore, we could do it because they didn't have time. We had no heavy equipment to do the work.

There were two or three areas of settlement on Point MacKenzie. One was remote—southwest of the military firing range for Fort Richardson, where we lived. The other two were north, nearer Goose Bay. One could drive to the north areas early on. One of the north areas was homesteaded by two brothers. They filed on land side by side. Where the property joined, they established their homestead dwellings. Both had "Jamesway Huts," a canvas building shaped like a Quonset hut used by the military and available at the surplus store. They were canvas over U-shaped whatchamacallits with flat ends for a door. They were cold and dark, but could be heated.

One family had three school-age kids and the other brother had one girl about twelve. To open a school it took ten kids, housing for a teacher, and a building to house the school. The Department of Education would supply all the material needed and pay the teacher. There were a few other kids who were to be included to make up the ten. The brothers were to build a school and they had a metal building they were going to use.

School started before the road got off the ground. The student body was the four children belonging to the two brothers and two other kids. I kept Butch also, because he was ready to learn to read. This was going to be a real old country school. A couple kids in fifth and sixth grade, a second grader, and three first graders—two very bright. The school supplies and furniture arrived, but no way or time to plan what to do with this group. Today there are good correspondence courses for kids that would have helped far more than the books used in a standard school setup where all the kids are close in what their curriculum should be, but we got just the standard materials.

I went up to the north side on September 21. School was to start the next day. The gentleman who was leasing the school building to the territory was working like a beaver on the building and asked Jack to stay and help. Jack missed the tide, so he decided to stay overnight. Our building owner, with the help of some homesteaders and other friends who had better sense, did a terrific job in getting that school building up. It was still unfinished, but we could get started. School was to start, the road was to go through, and the building was to be finished, all in the next few weeks. I was at the school and Jack was at the homestead. Both of us were lonely and frustrated. We didn't like being apart. We had lots to do at our place to make it livable. We were still camping. Jack is very gregarious and being alone wasn't what he wanted. I was trying to create a school in the middle of an unsettled mess where surviving the winter was first priority. No one had a decent place to live, it was hard to keep warm, the kids wanted the social life of town, we had no radio, TV or telephone and, on top of all that, winter arrived early, and with a vengeance.

Jack still had the boat in the water. As we got closer to winter, the boating became less pleasant; the wind blew more often, and, consequently, the water rougher. Jack came to the school as often as he could. He brought in the school supplies, including a first-aid book that showed how to deliver a baby. I'll bet I was the only teacher around who had a pistol in one drawer of her desk for protection from bears and a bottle of whiskey for first aid in another.

JACK

A weasel is not always an animal. In our case, it was the M29 Weasel, a light, tracked vehicle created for the military. They were designed to be able to quickly bolt up flotation tanks on the front and back of the vehicle. These tanks could be detached just as quickly. On land, Weasels were used to transport men or equipment over any terrain. Weasels were used in the Pacific for amphibious assaults.

After WW II, Weasels were surplused or sold. They became very popular in Alaska. Alaskans have adapted all kinds of vehicles so they could be used as ATVs—all terrain vehicles to the un-initiated readers who might be perusing this tome. They became very popular with hunting guides as a way to get clients from camp into the field and for bringing meat out. They were also great for homesteaders who didn't have road access into their homesteads. In our case, we had to drive one hundred forty miles from Anchorage, and then pioneer through a little over twenty miles of forests and swamps to get to our homestead. That wasn't really feasible. For getting people and stuff from the boat to the homestead, they were great.

I took a Weasel down to the beach to get the school supplies. I got the sled loaded and started to pull it back. The Weasel quit running. After a futile bit of tinkering, I walked back to the school. Next I took a John Deere cat and started back to the beach. While crossing the swamp, the cat got stuck. I decided to wait for a mother who would come to take her kids home from school. I figured I could use her Weasel to pull the cat out. At four o'clock, no mama. At six o'clock she came walking in, carrying her two small boys. She'd thrown a track.

Later I walked to the beach and tried to start the Weasel. Success! That machine purred like a woman in love being loved. Homeward bound. Just before I got to the school, the Weasel threw a track. Dave and I went to the Weasel the next morning and got the track back on ours and the mother's Weasel. We took both Weasels to the cat and got it out of the swamp. This was pretty typical. Everything took much longer than anticipated. Something was always breaking. Weasels were Army surplus because they were in need of lots of TLC.

Life at the school was rough. Because the road never materialized, Rita had to stay at the school. Of course, there weren't any quarters there so she had to stay in the school. We rigged a sort of pallet out of mattresses that could be picked up and put away during the day. She had to carry water about one hundred fifty yards from a community well, in a five-gallon can and she cooked on a camp stove. She always had a couple of our kids with her at night so she had to take care of them. The ladies would babysit during school. She had to wash dishes with no facilities for same. She had a Coleman lantern for light at night. Kids would wet beds, so there was that problem, also. The wood stove was very small. This meant wood was cut in small pieces and some had to be split. The stove couldn't burn for a long time so it had to be fed during the night, meaning no full night of sleep. She got pretty good at splitting frozen birch, but it was hard to keep warm. I had to come up every few days with food and, while there, cut enough firewood to keep the school warm. The base of the building wasn't banked, and the wind blew under the floor all the time. It took quite a bit more wood than it should have.

RITA

I remember one very stupid thing from my camping. I was alone in the school with my kids. It was dark so I had a lantern going. I looked at the lantern and noticed that the gas cap was crooked, so I undid it to put it on straight. I knew the gas was under pressure because I knew I had to pump it up. The flame shot up my arm. I still don't know why I wasn't burned, but I thank God that he looks after children and damned fools.

There are always funny things that happen even in the worst of times. The men homesteading in the cluster around the school were all in the Metal Workers Union. Most of them worked together. One had bought a small aluminum boat for commuting between Anchorage and their homesteads. This way, they could get home almost every evening. One evening, they were approaching the landing site and spotted a moose cow and half-grown calf on the beach right at the foot of the trail up the bluff. Bud Russell was running the boat and steered slightly beyond the normal landing spot in hopes that the two moose would move on up the trail. The cow did. The calf went into the water and started swimming toward the far shore several miles away.

The guys were sure that the young moose would never make that. It never occurred to them that, if they just landed the boat and got out of the way, the calf would swim back to shore and rejoin its mother. They went back out and tried to herd it to shore. No such luck.

One of the guys said, "If I go up on the deck and lasso it, maybe we can pull it to shore."

Bud said, "Give it a try." The other guy got a rope, fashioned a noose, and went up on the forward deck. Bud got as close to

83

the moose as possible and the guy lassoed it. They passed the rope back and tied it off to a cleat. They started to shore. The rope pulled the calf's head under the water. Bud slowed down enough for the rope to go slack. The calf swam up and tried to climb in the boat. Bud sped up. The calf went under the water. They repeated the episode several times. The calf rolled up on its side and quit moving.

"Hell, we've drowned it!"

"Get it to shore quick. Maybe we can give it artificial respiration!"

They got it up on dry land and pumped on it for forty minutes. They finally gave up and butchered it. Everybody ate veal for a few days. It never occurred to them that they'd strangled it, not drowned it. They could have saved the forty minutes.

JACK

Once the swamps froze, transportation became a lot easier. I was able to drive from Anchorage in to the school. Getting to and from the cabin was another matter. Of course, with the swamps freezing comes much colder weather. It was this colder weather that was the breaking point for the teacher and the school. Things were rather grim. They got grimmer, much grimmer. Finally, it was just too cold to continue trying to run a school with an un-finished building and everyone blaming each other for the lack of time. The situation was impossible. Rita and I went into town to resign her position as teacher. The local state superintendent was very understanding. He helped fill out the paperwork so as not to foul up her teaching career because of lack of housing. The people got a trailer for the substitute to live in when it was either housing or no school.

CHAPTER 14

JACK

About the time school started, Stuart, a good friend of ours, came over to spend a few days with Butch and me at the cabin. The day after we got home a wind came up. It got stronger and stronger. That evening it got so strong it blew the smoke down the chimney and into the room. We had to put out the fire and still couldn't see. The only way to keep warm was to go to bed.

The next day the wind had died and Stuart had to go home. Just before we three got to the beach, we met Loren. He looked very pleased to see us and said, "Boy! Am I glad to see you! I was just starting out for your place to see if you were alive! I was pretty sure you weren't."

Well, this greeting aroused my curiosity somewhat. "What do you mean, Loren?"

"I was walking the beach and I found a parka. Then I found the canvas off your boat. Then I found a rubber hip boot. Next I found your boat where the wind had sunk it. I started looking for tracks up the bluff, and couldn't find any. By the time I'd given up and started for your place, I was feeling pretty sick."

When I saw the boat, I felt pretty sick, also. Both engines were full of sand, both fuel tanks had been torn up, and a great log had stove in the deck and broken the transom. The boat was full of sand and all manner of debris. I was too sick to do more than look for a short time, but ....

We built a fire and flagged a plane. The plane radioed to Anchorage and pretty soon there was a helicopter from the rescue squadron at Elmendorf. Butch, Stuart, and I each got our first ride in a helicopter.

It took a week, and the help of several friends, to get the boat into town. I had borrowed Father Dumphy's boat the day after

Stuart, Butch, and I got to town via helicopter. We rescued the motors and got them into the shop for repairs. The day after I got the 40-horse out of the shop, I discovered the boat had sustained a little more damage than I had thought. To all outward appearances, the boat looked as though it was still seaworthy despite the damage already described. Joel and I loaded the boat with a ton or better of building materials, and started out for Point MacKenzie. The load was piled so high that at intervals I would have to stand on the transom to see over the load and make sure I wasn't running into ice.

I suddenly realized that the water was so deep in the boat, one fuel tank was moving slightly. I woke Joel up and set him to bailing. It was just a little tense, but Joel was able to keep slightly ahead of the water and by the time we reached shore, Joel had the boat almost dry. We unloaded the boat and I started back to town. Boy, what a time I had! I was steering with one hand and bailing with the other. Twice when I looked up over the deck, I found I was going around in circles. Finally the persevering and intrepid bailer made it to the dock. It seems that a hole had been punched in the bottom of the boat and a tarp had frozen over it. The prolonged trip across the inlet had caused the tarp to thaw out enough to leak. The total damage on the boat and motor ran over seven hundred dollars. Thank the Lord for insurance. So ended the last boat trip of the season.

I mentioned borrowing Father Dumphy's boat. He was a Catholic priest who brought a great deal to Anchorage. One of the problems in any small town is bored kids getting into trouble because there really isn't much to keep them occupied. Father Dumphy organized a club for teens with a focus on community service. He got a local laundry/dry cleaner company to donate coveralls for the kids. There was a popular TV series at the time called The Mod Squad. Father Dumphy took the coveralls to the church basement and stenciled "The God Squad" on them. Now the kids had a uniform. Their service projects included everything from sweeping sidewalks to helping older people winterize their homes. It wasn't long before non-Catholic kids were involved. Somebody donated a car and the kids with driver's licenses were picking people up and taking them to stores, church, etc. This is one of several great ideas that Father Dumphy put into action.

CHAPTER 15

RITA

Once we were back at the cabin, after the school was no longer my responsibility, we set to work getting settled in for the winter. That was quite a job. We had to put up the rest of the insulation, cut firewood, finish the basement, cut firewood, put up the "felt" (actually extra tar paper) on the outside of the house, cut firewood, build stools, a table, shelves, and a sink board, and oh, yes, cut firewood.

We had to put up an outhouse. Our outhouse, a "two-holer," was covered with a piece of tent to block the wind. It never has had a door. The plywood that was intended for walls was somewhere along the trail from the beach, covered with snow.

Ye Old Outhouse

Designed for a claustrophobic wife. Note the birch studs and the Styrofoam seats. This seat reflects body heat and improves winter use.

The longest walk in winter!

We concentrated on insulation first. I am, or at least was, so damn dumb. I wanted to make the insulation stretch, so I left gaps at both the top and bottom of each section. The insulation helped to keep the place warm, but not what it could have done if better installed. We still used wool blankets for sheets and slept in wool long johns. This was with two of us in a twin bed.

Jack built a table in the cabin so we could sit down together and eat. We had a kids' table and two little chairs that we had carried in, but wanted a big people table. The legs were two by fours and the top a square of plywood. Jack cut birch logs to use for stools. He cut triangles in one end to lighten them up so the stools could be moved around the cabin. The sink board was next. Jack used birch logs for uprights and two by twelves for a top. He dropped a sink into a hole he cut and placed a bucket under it for drainage. We had a bunch of boxes that white gas comes in, two five-gallon cans per box. We cut the boxes in half so that we could have four shelves for each box. We used a large box of oatmeal for spacing. The first set of boxes was an oatmeal box off the counter. The top half of the boxes was nailed to a length of shiplap lumber left over from the roof and floor. This shiplap was nailed to the wall studs. This second row of shelves was again an oatmeal box away from the first row. Those shelves were wonderful. One could see most everything in them all the time. They were deep enough for canned goods. We used a couple of whole boxes for the dishes and clothes.

Jack built the kids a "cute little boy closet" as Mike always called it. The rod, the trunk of a small tree, was down where the boys could reach it, and we had a closet with a higher rod. We built a wall of birch tree studs and cardboard between the kids' sleeping area and ours so the kids could be put to bed and sheltered from the light. The wall didn't go to the floor or ceiling to make it more efficient to heat the space. The top bunk was very cozy, the bottom one cold.

We used birch poles for studs. On the side of one of them, we started to mark the kids' height. When the grandsons came along many years later, they liked to compare themselves to their dad and uncles. There was a major forest fire after the grandkids were grown. Both daughters-in-law called to tell us we needed to charter a helicopter to fly in and rescue the story pole. It is no longer holding up the roof, but no one would use it for firewood.

We had left all of the furniture in the house in town so we could rent it furnished. We had no money and no way to get things to the cabin, so furniture was a luxury we couldn't afford. At the cabin we had beds and the kids' table and chairs—period. Everything else we created. Storage was a problem. We created a kitchen counter with a shelf under it. We used boxes from white gas cans for the shelves. Finally we could store dishes, pots and pans, and canned food. But now clothing was a problem. We didn't have lumber available to build shelves, and boxes really didn't work because you couldn't see inside them. Besides, we didn't have many. Jack and Roy were down on the beach when they found about six wooden ammo boxes that had floated in on the tide. They brought the boxes back to the cabin. I cleaned them out and we used them for clothes. But we still didn't have enough storage, and as they were only nine or ten inches tall, you could not see to the back.

One day while Jack and Roy were somewhere doing something, I decided to use the idea we had used to create kitchen shelves but to go one hundred eighty degrees in cutting up the boxes. So instead of cutting the boxes in two across the depth of the boxes, I cut the box into two pieces across the width. We had four saws, three I could use. We had a chain saw, a Swede saw for cutting firewood by hand, a handsaw, and a keyhole saw. I used the Swede saw to cut the boxes. It didn't cut straight, but it was faster than the other saws. I now had shelves ten inches by sixteen inches or so. I found six old, used two by fours left over from some building somewhere to use for legs, and spacers and whatever else a set of shelves might need. I tried to cut them the same length. I nailed the shelves to the two by fours, spacing them about fifteen inches apart. Driving nails into hard, old two by fours was a chore. I drove the nail through the box end into the upright, so no one would get scratched on the nailhead. Besides, I could use a smaller nail. I built the whole thing on its side. Getting it upright because of the weight was another challenge, but I did it. Now I had a set of shelves I could use for underwear and tee shirts. I put the socks in a small cardboard box and set it on a shelf. Things were up off the floor and one could see what one was after.

The thing rocked because the legs were not close to even. When Roy and Jack got back, they both started making fun of my endeavor, calling it a rabbit hutch, but Jack used it to attach a birch tree trunk for the clothes rack so we had a closet. That setup lasted for years until we added on other rooms and built closets with metal pipe for hanging coats and things that got left at the cabin. The rabbit hutch got moved into the tool storage area of the shed and is still in use today. Still called a rabbit hutch, also.

CHAPTER 16

RITA

We used melted snow for water. Many times each day someone went out and scooped up snow to fill all the pans that would fit on the stove. As the snow melted, the water in two pans were combined and one refilled with fresh snow. After we had some water, we strained it through a handkerchief to catch the birch seeds. We filled teakettles and milk cartons with water. One gallon of water was ten gallons of snow, so it took a lot of snow to drink, keep clean, do dishes and laundry. We always went to bed with pots of snow on the stove to melt and warm over night. We used the old rinse water to wash the next set of dishes.

We used Coleman lanterns that burned white gas for light. Each day the lantern had to be filled. We started the lantern as it was getting dark and went to bed when we ran out of fuel. One evening I was reading a book. The guy proposed and then the lantern went out. I tried matches and candles to find out what the gal answered. It was the next morning before I found out.

We had one large plastic mixing bowl. While I was at the school, Jack mixed pancakes in it. He didn't get it washed, so the batter dried up and stuck to the sides of the bowl. I worked very hard getting that bowl clean. I tried soaking and a little batter would dissolve. I tried scraping and a little more would come off. It took three or four days to get it clean enough to use. If I made pancakes in it, I rinsed it out right away even though we didn't do dishes until they were all dirty to conserve water.

There was a store in Palmer called Kosloski's. It had been established when the people were moved to Palmer in 1938 to start farms. It carried all kinds of things needed to live in the Bush, like heavy socks for kids. Our purchase there was a chamber pot. The boys would use an empty can and then we could dump it into the pot until morning when one could see to take the pot to the outhouse to empty it. The boys had been stepping outside to the nearest tree until Jack flew over the cabin after there was snow on the ground. He came in and stated that from that date forward he did not want to see yellow snow. I think that as time passed, the men learned how to go without leaving yellow signs. Maybe they stopped writing their names.

We had to wall the basement before we could spend time on the well. We were afraid the basement would erode out from under us. In February we had a Chinook, a southwest wind that is warm. This one was about thirty-eight degrees. I didn't know if it was good or not. We wanted a thaw to clear the land of snow so we could get it cleared at a lesser rate, but if all the snow melted we would have no drinking water, so we kept all vessels filled with snow just in case. Butch had gotten up one morning and looked at the tub I had filled with snow the night before to give the kids a bath. "Well, Mama, I don't know if it's warm, but it's water now, at least." was the comment. The water was like mud when I finished, but it had a hard life. First a bath, then wash clothes in a galvanized tub on a scrub board, and then the floor. No one can say I wasted water.

One very hard lesson for me to learn when living on the homestead was that clear, sunny days are cold. I would get up to a beautiful day and decide I had to get outside and take a walk because it was so pretty out. The sky would be blue without a cloud. The sun would be shining. Everything kind of glowed. I was always glad to come back inside because it was cold also, normally around zero.

CHAPTER 17

RITA

Jack was the one who went to town. He had to check in at the employment office to get his check each week, so at that time he took care of any business, the mail, and the shopping. He, Roy, and Joel would share a plane whenever possible. There was a flat fee for a round trip because the plane had to return to the airport. The pilot would buzz whoever was to be picked up, and the plane would land in the swamp between the three cabins. Then everyone tried to schedule things so Joel's return trip would be Roy's outgoing trip. This way the guys got to fly for half as much money as if the plane returned to Anchorage empty.

Jack could do some grocery shopping while in town, so we were able to have a more varied diet. I could bake cookies if I went over to Joel's to use his oven. One day Mike, Butch, and I went across the swamp carrying the ingredients for mincemeat cookies. Roy walked over with us. Every time we got near a tree, Roy would whack the trunk with his rifle butt and all the snow would fall off on me and the kids. The boys were delighted. We got over to Joel's and built a fire in the cookstove. I finally got my cookies baked, but only had half a batch because Roy was eating them as fast as I pulled them out of the oven. Then he told me to bake another kind next time because he really didn't like the mincemeat.

Mike, Butch, and I went over to Joel's a week later and again used his oven to make cookies and a cake. The kids had a great time splitting wood for the firebox. Each piece was about the size of your finger. I was able to regulate the heat by putting in one stick at a time. The boys saw this little tree near the window and decided to help Joel by cutting it down. We learned later it was still growing there because Joel liked it. We had cake and snow cream for dessert.

Another morning Butch was doing schoolwork and Mike was "writing a letter" to Grandma. He went and got an envelope. He folded the letter and put it in and asked me to put it up to go to town and be mailed. I said that he needed a name on it, meaning to address the envelope. So he took out the letter and printed, without any help, MIKE just as nice as you please. I was very proud of him! It was the first time he had ever printed his name.

Another time Jack took Mike to town to the dentist. They went to a deli that served hot turkey sandwiches and Mike wanted one for dinner. Both Jack and the waitress tried to talk him out of it because the serving was so big. But nothing else would do, so Jack let him order the sandwich. Of course it was turkey, stuffing, and mashed potatoes covered with gravy, cranberry sauce, a vegetable, a hot roll, and a salad. The kid ate every bite in an hour and a half. He didn't eat again for two days.

Whenever there was a heavy snowfall, the roof had to be cleared off to reduce the weight. Jack would set up a ladder and shovel the snow off the sides. Mike was up on the roof helping to get it clear of snow. He picked up a chunk and threw it off saying, "I'm going to kill you, Mr. Frazier."

Mike kept this up for some time until someone asked, "Why do you want to kill Mr. Frazier?" Joel always teased the kids, but he was never mean to them. Mike was hard to understand. He was three and had a speech impediment, besides.

His answer to the question was, "Mr. Frazier always says, 'You don't say.' And I do too say."

CHAPTER 18

RITA

While we had been trying to get the school going, our neighbors got settled in for the winter. Now they had time to play. Joel and Roy decided to go fishing. If they caught anything we would all have fresh fish for a change of diet. The two started out for Twin Island Lake, about six miles away, on snowshoes. They got there and set up camp. Roy had taken some plastic sheeting for a tent. They cut spruce boughs to put under themselves and went to sleep. It started to rain. When Roy woke up, he had a puddle of water between his legs held there by the plastic. Walking back was more than an ordeal. The snowshoes would no longer hold them up because of the rain and the sleeping bags were really heavy. Roy gave up and threw his sleeping bag away, but Joel carried his bag all the way back because it was new and expensive.

We had a celebration of Joel's birth on February 15. Everything and everyone got a little drunk out. The guys had promised the kids ice cream. Roy had a hand-crank freezer. Our roof sloped toward the south, catching all the winter sun. We had one and a half rows of insulation missing from between the roof joist because we had run out of fiberglass and it was so hot up there no one wanted to finish. Because of these two reasons, we had icicles hanging off the roof. The icicles tasted like oil because the roof was tarpaper, so they could not be used for drinking water. We used powered milk, eggs, and sugar and packed the bucket the ice cream container was in with the icicles and added salt. Watching guys with hangovers turning the handle on a freezer was quite a sight. They would bend over for a while and straighten up when the headache got too bad and let someone else take over. The ice cream was good. We ate snow cream whenever we had fresh snow, but this was better.

Of course winter wasn't over. We had a major snowfall. It was a winter wonderland outdoors. It snowed again that night. We all dressed and went out to cut firewood. Jack would hit a tree and knock all the snow off and onto the kids. They thought it was great sport. Of course anything a father does to play with his sons is usually fun.

One morning Butch got up and asked, "What is a snowstorm called?"

I answered, "A snowstorm."

" No," he said. "It is like an alligator."

I asked, "What?"

"Oh, I remember, a lizard." So that day we had a lizard and the sun was shining, too.

CHAPTER 19

RITA

Homesteaders are all interested in land, hopefully free. There were three designations of free land from the U.S. Government through the BLM. A homestead was a plot of land up to one hundred-sixty acres in multiples of forty acres. A cabin site could be no bigger than five acres. The other designation was a trade and manufacturing site, up to forty acres. If the land was already surveyed, one had to find the survey points and then prove up (meet the requirements to gain title or a patent to the land). Each designation had different requirements.

When the land had not been surveyed, the first step was to measure and mark with cairns each corner of the land that was wanted. A trade and manufacture site had to have an established business. A cabin had to be built on a cabin site. It could be small, more a shelter than a living abode. When these stipulations had been met, a person could apply for patent.

Roy and Joel wanted five-acre cabin sites over near Loren and Marcene's for duck hunting. One day Joel and Roy stopped by. They were going over to check Loren's family and lay out their cabin sites.

It had been a long time since I was away from the cabin and the kids. I was suffering from cabin fever, so I went with them and Jack stayed home to babysit. Both of the guys were on snowshoes, but I was just in boots. We did fine on the way over because we walked where the snow wasn't so deep that they couldn't pack it for me. But coming back I decided to take a short- cut through the trees up our trail from the beach. I guess it was about a quarter of a mile, but the snow was deep. I would take a step or three, and then I would break through the crust and fall a foot or so into deep snow. Then another few steps and another fall. By the time I got back to the cabin, I was covered with snow to my hips.

I got inside and decided I needed a soaking bath or I was going to be so muscle sore I would not be able to move the next day. We filled a round, galvanized tub with warm water and I tried to get in. We had brought this tub to be able to give the kids baths without giving thought to our being able to fit in it. We used it for a laundry wash tub also.

A major problem: I didn't fit. So I tried sitting Indian fashion, but the tub wasn't big enough for my feet and my "t'other" end at the same time. I felt like I could get stuck. Jack said he could pull me out, but he was afraid of picking me and the tub up at the same time. We certainly didn't want to spill all that water. He got the giggles so badly, I was ready to shoot him. He made a big deal of having to soap up my hips and fanny to get them slippery. There I sat with my fanny in and my legs out of the tub, trying to maintain my dignity, while Jack stormed about pretending he was looking for film for the camera. First, last, and only bath I took the whole time we were homesteading. Every other time Jack and I took a sponge bath with a small wash pan.

Joel, son number four, fit into the tub a whole lot better than I did

A couple weeks later Loren and Marcene and their two kids arrived at our place to return my visit. They had never been back here before. They brought milk and took back salted meat. We exchanged gossip and found out the firing range had been released. We talked about dropping our front eighty acres and picking up eighty acres behind us. Trade swamp for birch. I wanted to start a toothpick factory. While Loren was there, he witched us a well. He had tried in the fall but said at that time there was no sap in the twigs so they wouldn't work. Now as spring was approaching things should work better. Witching has always been quite a topic around water well drilling. The theory behind witching, or divining as it was also called, was that some individuals have the power to detect underground deposits of water. And these deposits can be found by using forked sticks or steel rods. The rods will turn toward the water. Loren had the power or ability to find water. He used forked sticks and walked around our cabin and in the basement. Loren felt the basement was a good spot and it saved seven feet of digging.

The kids went over to the jet while we visited. The jet the kids walked over to was an Air Force trainer that had crashed many years before. The Air Force had taken all the parts they could use right away and what was left was part of the fuselage. Many pilots knew about the jet and used it as a landmark. All the kids thought it was a neat spot. The seat was still there and one could climb inside and pretend.

CHAPTER 20

RITA

The weather started to warm up and no one had a well yet. It would be better to dig one in the winter because the sides would freeze at night and cribbing could be put in after the well was finished. Joel, Jack, and Roy, with the help of three little boys— one of them Roy's son, worked on a well for Joel. The first day it was down about thirteen feet. They used dynamite and hoped to hit water the next day. They hit water at eighteen feet in the late afternoon of the next day. The well digging had a side effect I didn't expect. My son, Mike, found he really could walk over by himself to visit Joel.

It is scary to look up and find one of your kids missing, but when you live in the woods and there are moose and maybe bears around, scary isn't a strong enough word. We had tried hard to let the kids have adventures, but I wanted those adventures to be where I could hear them. Mike hadn't been gone long when he and Joel arrived together. Joel wanted to be sure Mike made it back safely. He used the excuse that he only had one flashlight so he couldn't loan it to Mike to walk home.

In March, Jack and Joel started our well in the basement under the kitchen. Jack already had about six feet of the well dug before he got help. A couple of days into the digging they hit some very hard clay. It took a couple more days to get through the clay. At one point I sat on the handle of the post hole digger while Jack turned it, trying to get enough force to cut through. Finally, we had water, too deep for a pitcher pump, but good water. Joel and Jack put a barrel down as a crib in the well. We used a lard barrel from the bakery because the treatment was safe for food. It would be the bottom of the well and the well would be cribbed up from there. The rest of the cribbing was cedar. Cedar smells great and doesn't rot from getting wet, but boy, does it taste awful.

We were never able to just drink water. We added orange juice concentrate or Kool-Aid to cover the taste. We used a rope and bucket for access to the water. We stored food stuff in the bucket and removed it when we needed water. I developed quite a muscle pulling up buckets of water to do the laundry or water the garden.

The boys were out "helping" when Jimmy learned a new word. He'd learned to call Joel's dog, Tiger. Tiger had taken to knocking Butch and Mike down and then sitting on them and licking their faces. Jimmy, in the house, could hear them yelling, "Down, Tiger!" all the time, so he started yelling it also. At fourteen months, yet.

During the last few days of digging there had to have been up to one hundred little birds at a time coming to the dirt pile for grit. Jimmy would stand at the window and chatter at them as long as they stayed. We put up a bird feeder near another window. We tried everything to attract the birds and nothing worked until I noticed a bird pecking on the marrow of a bone the dog had. So Jack put the bone on the feeder and we had birds to watch. Those birds needed fat, not seed. Now we use sunflower seeds because of the fat content.

CHAPTER 21

RITA

We set the barrel stove at the center of the long wall, figuring that would give the most efficient heat radiation. We didn't have any experience or knowledge regarding "drafting" of a stove. We figured if the chimney went out the wall and turned up, we wouldn't have to worry about roof leaks around the chimney. That part was true. Everything else was downhill. Two ninety-degree turns in a stovepipe are hard to overcome in relation to draft. Also, birch contains a lot of creosote. The outside elbow got a huge collection of creosote and was a terrible fire hazard. We also didn't know that the top of the chimney needed to be several feet above a roof peak for efficient draft and to keep wind burble over the roof from creating a back draft in the stove. We found out all those things.

Jack had to go into town, got caught by bad weather, and couldn't get home. The wind kept getting stronger and stronger out of the south. The baby's crying woke me about five a.m. The cabin was full of smoke. I got up, opened the door, put the boys in my bed and climbed in with them. Our bed was a forty-inch bunk which Jack and I fit in quite nicely in those days, but it was really crowded with me and three boys. We got up at eight thirty. The room was pretty well smoke-free, so I closed the door. I was helping the boys get dressed when a gust of wind took the chimney off at the outside elbow. I had the stove closed down as tight as I could get it but it still puffed smoke into the cabin. I put outside gear on the boys and we went to Joel's. Joel said, "I've got another elbow and a couple lengths of pipe. I'll go over and see if I can fix things so the cabin doesn't completely cool off."

The wind was dying down really fast and Jack arrived right after Joel got to our cabin. It didn't take long to fix the chimney when one could see and had the stuff needed.

Eventually, we moved the stove to the west wall. This made it easier to have a kitchen corner and to have a straight shot for the chimney. We could have the top of the chimney above the peak of the roof so we had a good draft to the stove while the roof supported the run of pipe. It also got the stove away from the beds so it was cooler to sleep while melting snow for water and keeping the cabin warm.

CHAPTER 22

RITA

A major accomplishment of that winter was Jack's correspondence course. He was studying surveying from ICS (International Correspondence School) because a party chief made much more money than a chain man. He had been working on it for some time but something else always came first. At last he was ready to start the trig. He had been through four books of algebra and also one of geometry. He hoped to finish the trig in one month. After the math he had How to Survey, the part of the course he really wanted. Once he reached the trig, it all went pretty fast as it was easy for him and the end was in sight. Finishing a course like that is a major accomplishment. Only about one person in ten makes it.

When Jack dozed out the basement, he pushed the sand down the natural hill the cabin was on. So we walked up a slight rise and then down into the swamp. This made a great place to sled, and Jack and the kids would sled in the evening. It wasn't a long ride but guaranteed to make an old woman out of me just watching as they fell off at least three times on each ride. They had been using half of Loren's "Ahkio," a plastic sled developed by the Army to haul wounded when a stretcher wasn't usable. The hill in back of the cabin wasn't very long but had a tree growing close to the side. The goal was to get to the bottom without hitting the tree. The second goal: how far up the tree could you get the sled to go. The more the hill was used for sledding, the faster it got as the snow got packed into ice.

We still had to depend upon the weather for transportation. If the inlet wasn't ice-free and the swamp not satisfactory for a light plane on skis to land, one walked. Joel and Roy left Monday morning to walk to Goose Bay—twenty-one miles away. They were going to stop at Lake Loraine and fish. Somehow they missed the lake and ended up at the school Monday night. They got a ride from there to Anchorage in the back of a pickup truck. One hundred twenty miles is a long ride in an open pickup truck bed.

In the course of the winter Jack killed a moose for meat. We used every bit that we didn't share with our neighbors. It was the only meat that anyone had. The hunt was a community affair. Everyone got together and went hunting because none of us had any meat. The moose was butchered and hanging in our basement, waiting to be split among four or five families. A plane landed out in the swamp and two guys started toward the cabin. Well, the calendar was a little wrong to have fresh meat, so I quickly cleaned the rifle and hid it under the mattress on the bed. When the guys arrived at the door, we found out that they were relatives of a friend and wanted us to poach for them and sell them the meat. We managed to get them to go away but had no intentions of feeding them moose. We figured if you could own a plane, you could buy meat for your family.

We saved the moose hide and tried to clean it so we could use the hide for a rug. We scraped and used a wood rasp to get rid of the flesh. This rug was nice to step on rather than a cold floor when one got up at night. Our little black cocker spaniel also found it comfortable to sleep on, but in the night he was impossible to see so one would trip. The second problem was it was such good insulation it would freeze to the floor. Because we didn't tan the hide, it was always losing hair. This hair was a problem because it got into everything and was hard to clean up. The floor was so cold Jim was never able to crawl. He spent a lot of time sitting and walking around his crib, up off the floor, where it was warmer.

About this time of winter we went visiting, taking all the kids and walked across the swamp to Roy's house. We had dinner and played cards and, because it got late and we all had little company, we spent the night. We Stouts all slept in one bed sideways so we would fit. The next morning we walked home. A cold wind had come up overnight, so it was a long mile and a half. Then the cabin was cold because the fire had gone out. This was the only time we went visiting the whole three years we were living at the cabin. We would go for coffee but always came home to sleep.

In the middle of March the boys and I went to town. It was the first time we had been in town since the first of the year. I put Jim in the shopping cart as I walked around the grocery store. The kid's eyes almost popped out of his head. He hadn't seen people in so long that I think he forgot there were others out there. The people who had rented our house decided to go homesteading, so we had to clean it again and re-rent it.

In April Jack and Joel flew to town with Ray, another home-steader. Joel and Jack worked on the boat. They were hoping to get it into the water, but it got quite cold Sunday. Monday it was nine degrees and the tides were on the up trend so it was wiser to wait a bit to launch the boat. There was still a lot of ice out in the inlet. Dave's boat was in the water, so he brought them as far as the point and Jack and Joel walked back.

Shortly after the men left, a huge flock of Lesser Canadian geese landed in the swamp right below our cabin. They could have been headed for western Alaska or farther. The kids and I went up on the roof and watched them rest for a long time. No one was here to shoot one, so we have lots of geese to watch but none to eat. There were at least several hundred geese and the noise they made was unbelievable. The snow was almost all gone and the swamp had standing water everywhere that was eight inches to a foot deep. If you've ever been in a huge room full of people and they're all talking at once, then you have some idea of what I'm talking about in relation to the noise. We watched until the boys started telling me they were hungry and we climbed down and went in the cabin. Feeding them was easy enough, but I wasn't sure about getting them to bed. Even in the cabin the noise of the geese was awfully loud.

We had to have ten acres of land cleared within the first two years to meet our requirement for patent if we stayed fourteen months on the land; otherwise, if we stayed three stints of seven months, we needed twenty acres cleared. Of course there was a time limit and a fee to "commute" as staying fourteen months was called. We had contracted to have the ten acres cleared and had agreed to pay cash for the work. Many other people were willing to trade ten acres of land for ten acres of clearing. Because the school didn't work for us, our next obstacle was money. We had the house rented, so those payments were made. But we were too dumb to make the rent more than the payment, so we had no income other than Jack's unemployment, and most of that went for airfare to collect it. The rest went for food. Jack went into town to see about either selling or refinancing the house. We listed it for ten days and then refinanced it so we had the capital we needed. When Jack went to the bank to sign the papers, he was told we had a tax lien on our house. The IRS claimed that in 1948, when Jack was in high school, he had not paid his employees' withholding taxes. Now, how a boy in high school has employees earning enough money that FICA and ESC are withheld, was a minor technicality. Finally, the IRS decided it wasn't us and so we were able to borrow the money needed to pay for our clearing.

The snow was all gone in May. About this time we started to watch for Dave to move his cat in to clear our land. We figured he would come down while the swamp was frozen. Besides our ten acres, Roy and his dad were each going to get ten acres cleared and Joel was also clearing land. Dave was up by the school clearing land. We figured Dave had better start south soon or he wasn't going to get here. We really had no idea how long after the snow melted that the swamp would stay frozen. We have since learned it stays frozen into June.

In May, Jack and I spent two days laying out line to have our land cleared. We planned to have a triangle so we would be able to use it for a runway. We planned to have almost one thousand feet on both legs going into the big swamp. We would have a super-deluxe runway. After that all we would need was a plane! This runway was planned so that no matter which way the wind was blowing, a light plane could land safely. The cabin was in the middle of the two legs and all the middle where our garden was to be also counted as clearing.

Dave was to start south the next day. We wondered when he would arrive, because by then we realized that plans never seemed to happen on time. Dave arrived to talk about getting started with the clearing. He was going to be a few days more. We all had coffee and he went out and cleared a garden plot for us. He knocked down the trees and drifted them into a pile. Jack and I did the rest. We had to get rid of roots and cultivate with a garden fork before we could plant. The first day we worked a long time. The kids kept coming over to tell us they were hungry. Finally Jack said, "Why don't you go in and fix them a peanut butter sandwich, and we'll work until six thirty then stop for dinner."

I went into the cabin and came back out. I asked Jack what time did he think it was.

He said, "Oh, I guess it's about five p.m."

I laughed and told him it was nine thirty. So we all stopped and had peanut butter sandwiches for dinner.

We planted peas, radishes, lettuce, zucchini squash, broccoli, and collard. We were going to add potatoes, but not in this spot. By the time Dave got back to do the clearing, the squash was nicely up. After the trees were out of the way, the garden was in the sun all day. After a day or so, it was obvious that was too much sun for the squash, so we had to build sun shades out of the plywood that was to be used for the outhouse. Next, I built racks of string and poles for the peas. I found birch trunks about two inches in diameter. I cut them off about four feet long. One end was sharpened to drive into the ground. Next, I used kite string to make a netting for the tendrils. It took all day to get the job done. About four that afternoon a couple of very large helicopters came over. They circled the clearing to see what was happening down there. They blew over all my hard work. The next day I did it again. This went on every day. After the fourth or fifth day of rebuilding, I started to get prepared. This time, when I heard the helicopter coming, I went out to the garden. When the pilots started to come down to see what was going on, I started to throw sticks at them. I think they got the message because that was the last time my pea vines were blown down.

One day we went outside to water, and in the garden was a mama porcupine and her baby. Jack tapped the mama on the butt with his rifle barrel. She switched ends very quickly and if she had hit one of our legs, we would still be pulling quills. We chased mama out and she could waddle quite quickly. The baby trailed as fast as he could. Baby porcupines are cute—not cuddly, but cute.

We ate out of the garden until we went to town. I would go to the well, get a bucket of cold water, and then go harvest enough greens for a salad. The water was so cold it crisped the greens. Collard made a good salad green, tasting a lot like cabbage, and I would make slaw. We had salad a couple of times a day, not because we were short of food, but because everything was fresh and tasted good. Wilted lettuce with bacon was a favorite.

We got a small battery-powered radio. I would take it out into the garden to keep me company while weeding. There was a guy in Anchorage who would recreate the baseball games from the box scores. He managed to create a very exciting game and it was fun to listen. He even made up sponsors like martini-flavored Fizzes with dehydrated olives.

The reason for the radio was Mukluk Telegraph. This was a nightly broadcast where people could call in messages to be read over the air for people living in the Bush without a CB radio or phone. Mukluk Telegraph was from an Anchorage radio station, Glennallen had Caribou Clatter, and Fairbanks had something else.

110

Usually the messages were "I will be out on Tuesday if I can fly," or "See you when you get to town, as I made it safely." North of us were two high school girls who were spending a year in the Bush as their family was homesteading. The boyfriends would send messages and usually mention the Twilight Zone. The family had built the outhouse overlooking a valley, so while sitting there one had a beautiful view of the Twilight Zone. Half the people in Alaska were wondering about these messages.

The nicest thing about that garden was the rain. Carrying water from the well was hard work. First the water was pulled up hand over hand in a galvanized bucket. Then it was carried up the sand hill that was the front of the basement to the garden. Luckily for us, every evening just as we finally got around to watering, it started to rain. For the next thirty minutes or so we got a light rain; just enough to water everything, settle the dust, and get the kids inside.

It took a couple of days to clear the ten acres. Dave wore a mosquito net to do the clearing. The mosquitoes breed in the dirt so when it was disturbed, they flew. The trees would be falling and the birds darting all over, catching bugs.

Part of the clearing was finally a runway one hundred feet wide and one thousand feet long. We would use the berm for firewood, just as we had used the ones by the cabin clearing. We got news that Joel's mother was coming to Alaska so we had to get the runway ready. We picked sticks and I raked the whole thing with a garden rake. I couldn't move the next day.

After the land was cleared, it had to be cultivated and planted to meet the homestead requirements. Jack had gone to Ed Baldwin for seed. He got a combination of clover, rye and canary grass. He had a little sack seeder that hung over the shoulder with a handle to spread the seed. He walked back and forth across the clearing, spreading seed. Now with a little rain, we would have a hay field.

Joel's mother, Ollie, was one of those "strong" women who made America great. She was about sixty. Her husband, Joel's dad, was killed when Joel was a tiny baby. She worked to raise her child, at one time driving a long-distance truck during WW II. She had driven to Alaska to see her son because she didn't want to fly. She had her current husband, Joe, and another couple with her, and she did all the driving. Everyone was older than she and one of the others had diabetes, but wouldn't take insulin.

The only way to get to the cabin was to fly in to our runway or come over by boat and walk back two and a half miles. Ollie faced her fears and flew. Barton Air Service brought her over in a Cessna 180. When that plane landed it bounced three times, each one higher than the berm. It was such an "interesting" flight that Joel's mother went back to town in the boat. But our runway was now open. Of course there was a lot of work left to do and it took years to get it all done.

Jack and I met the plane, inviting Ollie into the house to wait for Joel. Joel could hear the plane at his cabin and we knew he would be right over. I was making coffee when I said something about hearing Roy's Weasel and that Joel would be along any moment. Her response was, "Is that what you call him?" So I explained what a Weasel was.

Jack and Joel took her fishing and she was more willing to slide down through the mud to get to the boat than to ride in another airplane. When Jack offered to help her, she told him, "When I need help from a young whippersnapper like you, I'll ask."

Jack went to work in June, staying in town, and I stayed on at the cabin until late August to finish our fourteen months of continuous living so we could "commute" our homestead requirements. Our kids enjoyed their life. Mike had an upside down birch tree standing in the berm with its roots toward the sky. We called the tree his Yertle the Turtle tree, for the Dr. Suess book he had gotten for Christmas one year. He could get up into the root

112

mass but Butch couldn't, so when Butch teased too much or did something else to earn his displeasure, Mike would climb up and then he could give Butch a bad time. The two of them wandered all over. We didn't seem to have any bears around. Maybe the kids made too much noise. There was lots of sand for little cars and trucks. They had a couple of swings that they made fly. But, at that point, I was ready to go to town to live where I could do the wash other than by hand and take a bath. It had been a good year, but I was glad it was over. We had finished up with all the requirements for homesteading.

We went back to the cabin that fall to harvest the potatoes we had planted on the side of the hill. We got about eight hundred pounds from the forty pounds we had planted, took them to town, gave lots of them away, and had potatoes all winter. Nice big potatoes. Digging up potatoes is hard, cold work. Someone pulled up the plant, and then the second person came along on hands and knees and sifted the potatoes out of the soil. By the time we got to that chore, the soil was cold to the touch so our hands got really cold. It always seemed to me that kids on probation should be sentenced to harvesting potatoes or cleaning up after a forest fire, something hard and unpleasant. It might be the motivation to stay out of trouble.

CHAPTER 23

RITA

We spent the winter in town. I taught school again, Butch went to school, and Jack worked.

About this time people were running for the first state legislature and senate. The state constitution had been approved by the voters before statehood was approved in Washington. Many candidates listed their qualifications as, "I have been in Alaska "X" number of years and I have "X" number of children." I have yet to figure out why having ten kids makes you a good legislator.

We were afraid that because we didn't get the initial clearing done within a certain period of time specified in the homestead law when Dave was a few days late getting started, we would have to cultivate a second ten acres. We were not going to lie on our application for patent. We decided that rather than clear land by bulldozing trees and to let the trees lay on the ground to rot, that we would drain the swamp by blasting a ditch from the creek that drained part of our place, across the swamp, and into Joel's homestead. This ditch was to be done with dynamite. It would be about one mile long. If we blew through the muskeg into the sand under it, we could create a drainage canal that would drain the land on either side of the canal. Once the land drained, we could disk and plant the muskeg and start to develop more tillable soil. Draining had been done in many areas of the U.S., so it wasn't a new concept. It just seemed wrong to doze up ten acres of trees, expose the soil to the wind, and not be able to farm crops because we couldn't get the crops to market because of a lack of a road. I figured it wouldn't take much time to blow this ditch and we could be finished with all our homestead requirements in about a month's time of working weekends. Boy, was I wrong.

CHAPTER 24

JACK

Once Rita and I made the decision to create a drainage ditch using dynamite, I had to go buy some. I went down to a supply house to talk about ordering. The owner happened to be working the counter when I came in. I told him what I wanted to do. He looked at me for a moment and what he saw was not reassuring.

"Have you ever done anything like this?"

"I've lived around dynamite jobs most my life, but the only dynamite I've ever used was in a mine when I was a kid." Well, I was twenty-five years old, but I looked like a kid to him.

"You worked hard rock?"

"Yes, sir."

"Well, that's 40 percent. You're going to need 50 percent for propagation."

I didn't want to tell him that I didn't have a clue what he was talking about.

"How long a ditch you gonna blow?"

"About a mile," I told him.

"All muskeg?"

"Yes sir."

"Okay, with 50 percent, you'll be able to get fifteen to twenty inches per stick. Fifteen's safe. You can try twenty, but if the muskeg's real dry you'll probably get skips. Stick with fifteen and you'll be safe." He started writing up the order. He looked back up at me as he was writing.

"You'll need forty-eight cases of powder and a box of caps. We bring our dynamite in from the igloo on Tuesdays. You can pick it up any time after ten," He slid the order form across to me and I signed it.

"Wait here a moment," he said and turned and walked away. He returned carrying two small textbooks on the use of dynamite. "Read these and bring them back when you come in to pick up the powder." I thanked him and left.

I went straight home and started reading. I found a chapter on propagation and found out it had nothing to do with progeny. It had to do with proper spacing between sticks so that one stick would set off the next one. I also found out that an "igloo" was a warehouse designed for storing explosives. It's conical and has heavy sides that get thinner at the top. The center of the roof is lightest. The idea is that if it blows, the blast goes straight up. This is supposed to cut down on damage to the surrounding area. When I finished reading everything that fit our project, I called my dad to discuss it with him. I wanted to be sure that I understood the texts well enough to do what had to be done without killing myself. My dad had worked some of the biggest rock jobs in history. This included one shot where they had almost two boxcar loads of dynamite in one hole.

Baldy and I picked up the powder and caps on Tuesday in his pickup truck and, when it was time to catch the tide, headed for the boat. We had the powder cases in the back and the caps on the front seat. We had the truck radio turned off. There is a theory that a radio transmission can set off electric caps. I don't think anyone's actually proved that, but that's why when you come to a road job where they're blasting rock, you'll always see signs asking you to please turn off your radio. We made one boat trip with the dynamite and one with the caps. I didn't want them both in the boat at the same time.

We got everything back to the swamp with the Jeep we borrowed and got it all stacked and covered to keep it dry. It was time to head back to town before we lost the tide.

On the way back to town, Baldy and I made arrangements to meet and start shooting the ditch.

"What time are you going back over?"

"I figure to go over Friday evening and start shooting Saturday morning."

"You bring the beer and grub, and I'll come with you."

"Sounds good to me. Let's meet at my house about seven. Tide's at nine. That'll give us plenty of time."

Saturday morning we started carrying each case of dynamite out and putting them at one-hundred foot intervals along the intended ditch line. We each put a case on a shoulder and waded off across the tundra. When we got where that box was supposed to go, we'd step out from under the box and let it fall. It finally dawned on me as I was watching Baldy drop his box that he was watching the box fall to see if it was going to explode when it landed. I then realized I'd been doing the same thing. I mentioned it to Baldy and we each got a laugh out of it. He said, "You know, if it went off, you'd only see it for part of a second."

I answered, "Yeah. Maybe we'd better start walking a little farther apart. That way, if one goes off, the other guy can tell people what happened."

Picture this: We were putting fifty pounds of dynamite on one shoulder and taking off. Each step was like walking on a coil spring mattress. Each foot would sink just past the ankle and there wasn't any stable support to bear our weight while we were swinging either foot forward for the next step. Doing this with your body straight up and down is hard work. Doing it with your body leaning to one side to compensate for the extra fifty pounds was a strain on your ankles and thighs that's hard to explain. By noon we'd walked back and forth along the ditch line enough times that we'd covered several miles. I looked at Baldy. He looked as bad as I felt. We started back to the cabin. There was

117

some good, cold beer in the well and we were both ready. "You got some aspirin back there?"

"I sure hope so," I said. We were both suffering from nitro poisoning. We both felt like somebody had hit us in the forehead with the business end of an ax.

Let me tell you about dynamite. Dynamite is sawdust that's been soaked in nitroglycerin, then packaged in a roll of paper. You can buy dynamite with as little as 30 percent nitro or on up. We were dealing with 50 percent. As long as the nitro is evenly distributed through the sawdust, it's pretty stable. Gravity will settle the nitro through sawdust. When storing dynamite, one has to turn each individual box over every so often because the nitro will settle to the bottom side of the sticks. You turn it over so that it starts back toward the other side. If the nitro is allowed to puddle, it liquefies and becomes very unstable. I had all that explained to me by my dad when I was thirteen. I'd found a stick in an old mine and carried it over to my dad to show him. He held his hand out and said, "Lay it in my hand very gently." I did, and he very carefully set it on the ground. He took my arm and we walked away thirty feet or so and he turned around and shot it. There was an impressive amount of noise, we were pummeled with some sand, and then he explained just how dumb I'd been. I'd also been very lucky. The paper wrap on that stick was so saturated with nitroglycerin and so oily that I was carrying it by one end with just my thumb and one finger. It could have gone off as soon as I picked it up. I was lucky that I had a dad who was cool enough and wise enough to do exactly what he did. That was my first lesson about handling and storing dynamite.

Some people are very susceptible to nitro poisoning. Baldy and I were two of them. When working with nitro, you absorb it through the skin. As soon as it gets in the bloodstream, it stimulates the heart enough to create a terrible headache. Baldy and I drank our beer and crashed. I did find some aspirin. It finally took effect and we started back toward feeling human. When I felt safe trying to put thoughts into words, I asked Baldy, "You know anybody in town that might have a Weasel for sale? It's obvious that this won't work." Baldy had sold his Weasel the previous year.

"Yeah, John had to give up guiding. He's probably still got a couple."

"Let's have something to eat and go find John." We were able to find a Weasel and negotiate a price I could afford. Getting it to the homestead was another matter. We borrowed a trailer and towed it 120 miles around Knik Arm to the end of the road. Baldy started in with the Weasel. He had a little over twenty miles to go. There were two major tidal creeks he had to ford and a lot of places where the trees were so thick and high that he had to trust his ability to maintain directional control. I turned around and started back to Anchorage. I had to return the trailer, launch the boat and go pick up Baldy. We figured we'd both get to the homestead about the same time. I beat Baldy by a little over two hours. I have to admit I was a little concerned by the time he showed up. The Weasel made all the difference in the world. Being able to put the powder in the Weasel and take it where it was needed reduced our workload about 80 percent.

We established a straight line across the swamp by deciding where we wanted to go and then setting three poles in a line. As we approached the first stake, we'd move it ahead of the last stick in line. This way, we always had three stakes to line on and it made keeping a straight line a cinch. We placed the powder by working a stick down into the muskeg about three feet and then pulling it out. Then we'd drop a stick of dynamite down the hole and plug the hole. We "capped" the last stick of dynamite in the box. Capping is done by poking a hole in the end of the dynamite and inserting a dynamite cap in the hole. Then the electric wire leads going into the cap are wrapped around the stick a few times, and the stick is dropped in the last hole.

The lead wires bonded into the caps were twenty feet long. Our main wire was one hundred feet long. When we were set up to shoot, we were one hundred twenty feet from the near end of a string of one hundred ten sticks of boom. Each blast would throw up an impressive line of debris. It included chunks of muskeg, various sized pieces of root material, and lots of water. Anyone watching would see a line of swamp 150 feet long suddenly rise one hundred feet or more straight up. We quickly learned to be on the upwind side of the ditch or get sopping wet with very black, organic guck.

It took us most of the summer to shoot that darned ditch. Every weekend, we'd go over in the boat on Friday and work as late as we could until Sunday and still catch the tide to get back to Anchorage. I was working in town ten hours a day, five days a week, and then we went to six tens. That cut down even more on the time I had to go over. Rita and I worked out a system. We discovered she does not get headaches from handling dynamite. I would poke the holes, Rita would drop in the dynamite, and Butch, our eight-year-old, would plug the hole by tamping muskeg down into it. Our system sped progress a great deal.

Rita was about "12½-months" pregnant at this time. We were almost done. We really pushed that last day and shot five or six cases of powder. We were finally done and cleaning up when Rita turned to me and said, "If we ever write a book about this, we're going to call it *To Hell With Togetherness*.

There were several funny things that happened during the work. I rigged up a little blasting machine that held two D-cell flashlight batteries. It was light to carry and had plenty of power to set off the caps. The first time Butch was down on the ditch line with me, he wanted to set off the shot. We got all set up. I let him hook up the blaster and told him to shoot when he was ready. He pushed the button, spun around, handed me the blaster with a "Take it, Daddy, quick!" And he started running. I don't think

Boxes of dynamite to be used on ditch. The boxes were moved from the boat to the top of the bluff and then back to the edge of the swamp where they were handy to the "ditch" in progress.

Pulling a shot. The muskeg went into the air about 200 feet. Root mass was blown out clear down to the sand that had once been a lake bottom.

121

he even saw his first shot. I guess when he'd been standing up by the cabin watching the other shots, they'd made quite an impression on him. Another day we were all ready to set off a shot, the blaster was in my hand and we could hear a plane coming. We couldn't see it because of trees. Just as he appeared, I shot. The only problem was that he wasn't five hundred feet up like he was supposed to be. He was maybe three hundred feet. It must have looked like the whole world was reaching up to grab him. He was at five hundred feet in very short order.

A good friend, Dave Harper, came over one day to watch. By then, I was using the battery in the Weasel to shoot the powder. We were one hundred feet from the ditch line, standing beside the Weasel, and I was about to touch the wires to the battery. Dave was looking in the Weasel at ten or twelve cases of dynamite. He looked back at the ditch and back in the Weasel. "Jack, are you sure it's safe to be this close with all this other dynamite?"

"Dave, I've been doing it this way all along." Dave's only experience with explosives had been from twenty thousand feet up while he blew up half of Germany.

"Well, why don't you wait until I get a little farther from the Weasel?"

"Okay, go for it." And Dave took off towards the downwind side of the ditch. When he got about as far on that side as I was on my side, he turned around and hollered, "Shoot!" I shot.

Dave watched that mass of goopy stuff rise up and up and start right for him. I'll say this for Dave. He didn't put his head down and run. He stood up to what he had to do. He kept his head up, kept watching, and kept dancing back and forth, dodging all the big chunks coming at him. He dodged every darned one! When he came back to the Weasel, he looked like the creature from the black lagoon. Everything was black but his very white teeth.

He was laughing! "Boy," he said, "did you set me up!" We went back up to the cabin so he could clean up.

RITA

I had been keeping a daily journal. Actually it was more of a "when I thought about it and had time and something to write about" journal. In the back of my mind, I figured someday I would write a book using the journal as a starting point. While working out in the swamp helping with the dynamite, I decided that just maybe we could be the plot of a TV series like the Beverly Hillbillies or Ma and Pa Kettle Go Homesteading. A very pregnant woman in knee boots, planting sticks of dynamite could shout something like, "To hell with this noise, no more togetherness for me!"

I was greatly frustrated because that dynamite came in cardboard boxes. Jack had always talked about all his family had done with the boxes that had been packed with dynamite, how people had made furniture from them. We had used gasoline and ammo boxes, and I had all sorts of plans for forty-nine wooden dynamite boxes.

Mike was the daredevil of the family. He would ride on the top of the roof of the Weasel while Butch rode inside, at least at first. Mike was also the one who wanted to pull the shot.

Sometime before Joel was born, Roy was with us at the cabin. We took the boat back to town. The wind was blowing and the water was rough, so we decided to wait until the tide changed to see if the water would calm down. Cook Inlet and Knik Arm have no wave action, so when one sees white- caps, one with good sense stays on land. The tidal change seemed like the end of the whitecaps, so we decided to head for town rather than go back to the cabin for the night and have to get up early to go to town. I remember saying to Roy, "If anything happens, you have to save the kids because I can't swim." As we got nearer the point, the water developed into a rip. A rip develops when two primary currents come together. If the wind has created wind action, the waves from each current crash into each other and they explode straight up. In this case, the waves in each current were running about three feet high and when they collided, they exploded into a column of water five or six feet high and six to ten feet in diameter. Jack was timing these explosions so the boat would arrive at one just after it collapsed. At one point his timing was off and the thing picked our boat right out of the water. We were balanced on top with both propellers out of the water and the boat was being carried toward some rather large rocks.

Roy yelled at Jack, "You better do something!" Of course there was nothing to do until the propellers were back in the water. The water column finally collapsed in what was probably thirty seconds, but seemed like thirty years.

When we got to Anchorage, Jack looked at me and asked, "What were you saying to me out there? I couldn't hear you."

My answer, "I wasn't talking to you. I was praying." Once again God looked after those damn fools and children.

CHAPTER 25

RITA

There was still a little bit more swamp to open up, but Jack wasn't there to do it. Joel had never set off dynamite and I really had only watched but .... We took a box of powder, a cap or two, and a remote controller from a car the kids had. The controller took two D-cell batteries to make the car go forward and backward. Jack had used this device in the beginning of ditch blowing. We walked down the trail to the spot where we had corduroyed the swamp. I explained how to poke the hole into the ground, plant the stick of dynamite, cover it with sod, and measure to the next spot. We got the sticks into the swamp and placed the cap into the last stick. We got the wires hooked up and then went over behind a clump of brush and touched the wires together. Nothing happened, so we wiggled the wires and tried again. Still nothing. Neither knew just what to do. Leaving the dynamite in the ground wasn't a good idea. So we both stood up and discussed the situation. We knew we could plant a second stick and cap, but weren't sure what that would do.   Finally we re-hooked the wires and tried again. This time we just stood at the edge of our line of sticks. Now it worked and the ditch was closer to open. Joel, being a gentleman and deciding I had no business setting off sticks of dynamite, sent me back to the cabin and he finished the work for the day.

Later Jack used the Weasel to disk and, using a hand spreader, seeded the ground on either side of the ditch. The planting of the swamp gave baby Joel, our fourth son, his first plane ride. We had Barton Air Service fly us over to the point. Joel was ten days old when we went back to plant. He slept in a banana crate. That was when Bill Barton showed us how to pick up a small baby by the middle of its back to relieve pressure on its ears. "Let me show you guys something." He took the baby from me and laid him on a desk on his back.

"Slide your fingers under the small of his back and gently lift him until his head tips back without actually removing support. This seems to open their ears and relieve the pressure created by landing." We've used that trick for years and shared it with many mothers on commercial flights.

JACK

I'd been working all summer up the highway towards Glennallen. We had two sites under construction. One was at Milepost 120 and the other at Milepost 164. These were microwave towers and related structures. This was some of the most famous hunting country in the Western Hemisphere. There were moose, sheep, grizzly bears, caribou, and wolves. That was just for starters. Then there was the beauty of the country. Fantastic alpine vistas, wild rivers, glaciers and, overlooking everything, bare granite peaks sticking up so high that God uses them to scratch his back. By August all I could think about was getting our Weasel up there for hunting season.

A couple of friends on the job, Gene Oaks and Al Benson, and I devised a scheme to get it there. I was far enough ahead with my work that I could take Saturday off without messing up the construction schedule. The company had a two-ton truck up there for a job truck. We talked the superintendent into letting Gene take the truck into Anchorage Saturday evening. He'd meet me with the truck at the trailhead at Goose Bay Sunday evening. We'd load the Weasel into the truck and head for the job. All I had to do was get twenty hours of work done at the homestead, walk the Weasel cross-country twenty-some miles, and meet Gene about six o'clock Sunday evening. Not a big deal for Super Jack.

I drove home Friday night. Rita and I and the boys flew over early Saturday and went to work. Everything went as planned. We got the work done. I put Rita and the kids on the plane to Anchorage and I started north. Eighteen miles into the trip, I came to the edge of Goose Bay Flats. This is a huge tidal basin five miles across and twelve miles deep. Like all tidal basins, it had tidal sloughs running everywhere. There was a trail across about seven miles long. This trail was only good during low tide. High tide was at eight this day and it wasn't quite five. I had plenty of time and the Weasel was running well. I had it made. I was two hundred yards into the flats when the right track broke. I managed to get up on a low hummock that, hopefully, would keep the rig above high tide. Now I'm in big trouble! I didn't have the right tools or the time to fix it before the tide would get me. I took my three rifles that I had along and at five thirty, I started running for the far side. I made my way through the first two sloughs along the trail before the tide shut off that option. From that point on I had to work my way around what sloughs remained. I got to the trailhead, just across the flats at nine thirty. The most beautiful sight in my world was a big red truck with Gene Oaks sitting in it! In four hours I had run and slogged thirteen miles, carrying three rifles and about thirty pounds of gear. I don't remember ever being so exhausted before or since. Gene took my gear and stowed it for me, then helped me in the truck. He drove to Palmer, woke me up, got me into the restaurant of the little hotel there, ordered hamburgers for each of us, got us rooms for the night, poured a boilermaker down me, and I vaguely remember him helping me out of my filthy clothes before letting me fall on the bed.

Monday evening I called Baldy. "Hey, Baldy. I left the Weasel on the south side of Goose Bay Flats with the right track busted. Have you got time to go fix it?"

"How bad's it broken?"

"The primary cable on the outside."

"That's it?"

"Yep. If it had been anyplace but the tide flats, I'd've tried to ease it on in."

"What do you want me to do with the Weasel?"

"It's got plenty of fuel. Take it on back to my place. You can have Barton pick you up there and I'll pay him when I get back to town."

"Okay."

"Call Bud Russell and ask him to run you up in his boat. He's just dumb enough to offer to help."

"Sound's like a plan."

"Thanks, Baldy, I owe you." It helps to have friends that you never have to look around to see where they are when the stuff hits the fan. Baldy's the kind of guy that'll be right beside you no matter what. He'll do to ride the river with. He did, in fact, fix the Weasel and walk it back to the homestead for me.

There's one more thing I want to tell about while we were building that tower. We were staying nearby at Meekin's Lodge. Austin Meekin was a very famous big game guide. He hunted with horses to get into the back country. The weather was horrible on this particular day. You couldn't see the mountains because the clouds were too low. Visibility was fifty yards because of rain. Ducks weren't even trying to fly. We'd gone back to the lodge for lunch and a chance to be inside and breathe without scuba gear. Well, you know, the weather was really, really bad! Gene and I had finished eating and were standing out on the gallery that ran across the front of the lodge. Suddenly, Austin came riding in with two hunters plodding along behind him. The only thing I've ever seen that looked more forlorn than those three guys were the horses they were riding. Austin had water running off the rim of his Stetson all the way around. He looked over at Gene and me.

"Don't you so-and-sos stand there grinning at me!" He jerked his thumb over his shoulder, "These guys are paying me ten thousand dollars to be out in this!!"

CHAPTER 26

RITA

Anchorage had a new superintendent of schools. He changed the rules. Two years before, I taught up until Jim was born, eight days before in fact, and stayed off six weeks and then went back to work. Now, I was supposed to quit at four months of pregnancy. I couldn't count well, so I worked through the end of the school year. I was then required to stay off six months. Joel was born in August, so I was to be off until February, and then who knew where I would go or what I would teach as my school would not be guaranteed until September. Jack had been working for the City of Anchorage and got laid off in October. As a government agency, the city didn't pay employment insurance, so Jack could not draw unemployment compensation. Things looked pretty bleak; we hadn't planned for the layoff. We had finished all our requirements for homesteading, but we could go back to the cabin and rent out the house again and not lose the house for lack of money. We found an electric stove for the house so we could take the propane stove to the cabin, a double bed, a small crib for Joel, a generator, a wringer washer, and a set of portable washtubs. Now we could do the laundry—hanging it to dry—bake bread, and sleep in something besides a twin bed. This also meant the three boys would not have to sleep in one twin bed. Jack took the furniture across the inlet in the boat to the beach as winter set in, and then dragged it on a sled back the two and a half miles to the cabin. Getting the propane tank up the bluff was quite a feat. It weighed close to 200 pounds.

After all the furniture was in place, I took all the money we had to the grocery store and thought I was buying a year's supply of food. I packed it all into egg crates. No one could move the crates because they were so heavy. Jack arranged for a friend to fly Mike, Jim, Joel, and me over to the cabin to join him, Butch and the dog. Jack's friend, Pat, had a Super Cub, a small two-place plane.

First he flew the food over to the cabin and then us. I sat in the seat with Mike on my lap, Jim on Mike's lap, and Joel in front of Jim. Pat took off and banked to turn, Jim popped up and I said, "Sit still, Jimmy." Pat banked some more, Jim popped up and I said, "Sit still, Jimmy."

About then Pat figured out what was happening in the back seat. Jim was sitting on the stub of the stick that let a person in the rear control the plane. This stub moved when Pat banked to turn, and Jim moved because he was getting poked in the butt. Of course, Jim was making it much harder to turn. After the second, "Sit still, Jimmy," Pat hollered, "Stand up, Jimmy," and we flew around the control tower instead of into it. We landed at the cabin, unloaded, and settled in for the winter.

CHAPTER 27

JACK

Back in July or early August before Joel was born, I was working up the highway 130 miles out of town. I had taken off a little early on Saturday and had come to town to spend the night with my family. I got a ticket for rolling through a stop sign. I had to be back at the lodge where the crew was staying Sunday night. I gave Rita the ticket so she could pay it for me. That inconsiderate female had a baby instead of paying the ticket. Months later, I was in town to collect my unemployment check and get our house ready for a new tenant. Baldy's wife, Laura, was in town and trying to get back to Point MacKenzie. The weather was terrible right then and she called me to see what I thought about catching a plane out.

"Nobody's going to fly in this. But I'll tell you what. If you'll help me clean this house, I'll buy you dinner and we'll fly home together first chance and share the cost of the plane."

"It'll have to be a steak dinner."

"Deal!"

We'd been working about two hours and had worked our way from the kitchen, through the living room, and were in the back bedroom. I went out to the kitchen to get more rags. There was a knock at the front door as I was going back through the living room. I opened the door and there were two cops standing there.

"Are you Jack Stout?"

"Yes."

"Sir, you are under arrest. You'll have to come with us."

"You've got the wrong Jack Stout. I haven't done anything to be arrested for."

The cop who was talking backed up enough to read the address by the door. "Jack Stout, 1404 West 44th Avenue."

"Fellas, why don't you both step inside and let's try to figure out what's going on."

They came on into the house. "Sir, you were ticketed for running a stop sign and you've never paid the fine. After ninety days a warrant is automatically written for an arrest."

"Oh, man! I thought my wife had paid that. I was working up the highway and had to be back there Sunday. She said she'd pay it, but she had a kid instead. Am I actually going to jail?"

"No, you pay the fine and we'll bring you back out here."

"What about I follow you in, pay the fine, and you don't have to bring me back?"

"That's good for us."

All this time, Laura was blissfully working in the back bedroom. I turned to face the hall.

"Hey, Laura," I said in a loud voice. " I've been arrested. I'll be back in a little while."

Laura, of course, thought I was kidding. She was going along with the gag.

"Oh, no, you don't." She bellowed, "You're not going off and leaving me to clean this house!" and she came charging out to the living room. Laura was 5'10" and weighed about 200 pounds, a big hunk of woman. When she charged into the living room, it was America's funniest moment in time. The cop nearest to her actually jumped back. Laura's face went totally blank and she said, "Oh" in a little, tiny voice.

If I'd have gotten a picture of that moment, I probably could have gotten the cop to pay the fine for me, and I wouldn't even have had to go downtown with them.

CHAPTER 28

RITA

The year we were gone, Roy had improved his cabin. He had added a room or two, put in a cesspool and a drain from the kitchen sink. He fixed up his sink so he had running water from a barrel he could fill and built a chicken coop, to name a few improvements. Roy had put up paneling, so he brought over all the cardboard he had used as walls in his cabin before the paneling, and we stapled it up onto the studs. Made the place much warmer. Jack and I would work on the cabin—most of it outside closing in the basement. Jack set spruce piling along the side of the basement. Then he used his saw to cut trees lengthwise to make walls. These got worked between the dirt and the piling. Then dirt was pulled down to hold the split log in place.

The groceries didn't last as long as planned. The family had moose to eat. Neighbors shared an animal because no one had refrigeration. Someone would kill a moose and all would share. One morning there was a knock on the door and Demaris came to get Jack to help her dress a moose she had shot. Jack took Mike and went along with Demaris back to her place. It turned out it was a pregnant cow, so along with a lesson in how to field dress a moose, Mike wanted a lesson in biology.

We had a frozen hind leg of moose hanging in the basement. We would carry the moose up the bank and into the cabin where we used either the power saw or a handsaw to cut off portions for a few days' meals. Then we carried the moose back into the basement. We figured that if the butchers used saws to cut frozen meat, we could, too. Our saw had a reciprocal blade instead of a lubricated chain of a chain saw, so there was no oil to get on the meat.

CHAPTER 29

RITA

Right before Christmas, Ruth O'Buck, one of the pilots from Barton Air Service, landed in the swamp below the cabin and walked up to the door and knocked. She announced, " I have groceries for you." We knew we had not ordered groceries, but she insisted that the food was for us. Jack went back to the plane with Ruth to unload it. The only seat in that plane was the pilot's seat. The other three had been taken out to make room for food! There were boxes of food stacked right to the top of the plane. They got the plane unloaded and Ruthie said, "I'll be back as quick as I can with the next load." It seems that the teachers at the school where I was teaching knew how broke we were. Every school collected food for others for Christmas. Usually it went to the Salvation Army for their food baskets. These two gals decided that our family could use the food as much or more than the Salvation Army, so they arranged to send it to the point along with a present for everyone, including a toy for each child. There was a complete Christmas dinner, as well as staples.

When Jack got both plane loads up to the cabin, we had a huge pyramid in the center of the floor. Jack went over to Ed and Demaris's cabin and invited them over to help sort stuff according to the needs of each family in the area. They came back with him and we spent the rest of the evening playing Santa Claus sorting his pack. It was a blast. One pile was for Ed and Demaris, primarily staples. One pile each for Roy's house and our house. These were foods for easy extending of meat and snacks for the kids. There were two cases of canned milk. Because Joel was being nursed, we gave one case to Roy for baby formula, the other went into Loren and Marcene's pile for baking. We knew that they were out of oatmeal, sugar, flour, and dried fruit. They got the lion's share of that stuff because Marcene's favorite thing in life was baking. We loaded Ed and Demaris' groceries into the Akhio and they went home with promises to be back early in the morning to help Jack deliver the other things. Said delivery involved a walk of ten miles. At least it was all on well-packed trails and no snowshoes were needed. Ed had his heart set on going and that meant a very slow trip. He had angina so bad that half the doctors in Anchorage prescribed nitro pills for him. Ten miles would take up to two hundred pills for Ed. It was an all-day event.

All the people living on the point got together at our house for Christmas dinner, which included turkey with all the trimmings. Some of the things that came in on that plane are still there at the cabin, like a doll that Jim got and a fruitcake can.

That food kept us all going until the seismograph company came into the area and there was employment to be had.

JACK

This was the Christmas before Mike's sixth birthday. Butch had gotten his .22 the Christmas before his sixth birthday. Mike was firmly convinced that a tradition had been established. I had, in fact, bought a rifle for Mike. It was the same model as Butch's. I'd also gotten an extra rifle stock. The idea was that I could switch the stock on Butch's rifle with the one that came with Mike's. If the full-size stock was still too long for Butch, I would have a third stock that I could cut to an eight-year-old size. I figured that would give me two short stocks for each boy when he was six. They'd also have a full-length stock for when they grew into it.

When we got the tree up, Mike's rifle was one of the first things under it. I figured we'd get away with that because the rifle was unassembled in the box and the box was much shorter than an assembled rifle. The box was gift wrapped in such a way that nothing of the box was visible. Mike came charging through the door a few minutes after the rifle was placed under the tree. He stopped dead in his tracks. "That's my rifle!" he said.

"No, Mike, that's something for your mother."

"Oh, no, Daddy. That's my rifle!"

I got Butch's rifle off the rack and held it up to the box. "See Mike? A rifle won't even fit in the box."

"That's my rifle!" And a very excited little boy went charging out the door to tell his brothers about his rifle. It's a damned good thing there was a rifle in that box Christmas Eve. Rita and I might have died in our sleep.

I've got to tell you about the Christmas tree. When it was time, we all trooped out into the woods to find a tree. We found a spruce that was perfect in shape. It was at least six feet too long to fit in the cabin. We got it down and dragged it back to the cabin. I measured the radial distance of the tree and went in and set that distance from the wall. Then I measured the distance from the floor to our sloping ceiling. I went out and cut the tree six inches shorter than the distance to the ceiling. We took it in and tried it.

Rita said, "How are you going to stand that thing? It's too big for this little cabin. Between the boys and the dog, it'll get knocked over several times a day."

"I'm not going to stand it. I'm going to hang it." That's what we did. It swung and it spun, but it never fell over. From that time on, wherever we lived, there was a cup hook in the ceiling just out from a corner in the living room from which we hung the Christmas tree.

CHAPTER 30

RITA

Because Loren and Marcene were planning on making the Point MacKenzie area a permanent home, they knew they had to live off the land. They had seed for everything that would grow and seed for things to experiment. Loren used logs to build raised garden plots to grow corn and tomatoes. Marcene planned to can all the vegetables that grew that couldn't be kept in a root cellar. She had a large pressure cooker, a sealer for the cans, and washed out all the cans so they could be used again.

One of their first acquisitions was a cow for milk. Using modern science, they had bred the cow. When it was time for the calf to be born, Loren had rigged an intercom between the shed the cow was in and the bedroom where he was sleeping. No one wanted a bear to get the calf. Marcene woke to sounds of the cow kicking down the shed. She woke Loren and he went out to shoot a bear. It wasn't a bear that caused the problem. It was Loren. He had reversed the intercom and the cow panicked when she heard Loren snoring.

We took the boys to see the calf and I got to see the new house. Before the family moved to the point, Loren had built a small log cabin. The family lived in that until time was available to build something better. After Loren and Doyle hauled in the sawmill, they had cut down spruce trees and, using their sawmill, cut the trees into lumber. They had a small house with rooms. Loren used the sawdust for insulation. Marcene also had a kitchen with two stoves, a wood-burning one and a propane stove for baking and canning.

Life went on for a time. Butch, a third grader by then, went to school at the kitchen table. He didn't really like schoolwork so we came up with a reward system. For every A or 100, he got two .22 shells for a reward, a B was only one, and below a B—nada.

We also worked out a system where he got all his assignments on Monday for the week. The sooner he got them done, the more time off he had. Often he had four day weekends.

JACK

Butch was permitted to shoot at targets whenever he wanted, and he had a trap line near the cabin set with rabbit snares. Butch tried to talk me into letting him go rabbit hunting by himself the winter he was eight. We reviewed all the safety rules that included being sure he was facing away from any cabins before he took his shot. I finally let him go all by himself with five bullets. He came home with one rabbit. The only one he saw. He came in very proud of himself. He stood in the doorway and held it up for everyone to see. He also held it so we could see that he'd shot it in the head. Then he made a mistake. He tried to talk his mother into cleaning it for him. I went out with him and talked him through the dressing.

"Always open up an animal just as soon as you can. The sooner it starts cooling, the better the meat."

"Yes, sir."

"How many bullets did you bring home?"

"None, Daddy. You told me to shoot them in the head so I wouldn't waste meat. It took me all five to get him in the head."

"What was the rabbit doing while you were shooting and reloading?"

"Hopping around."

"You'll do better next time. I'm proud of you. You did fine."

RITA

Jack's birthday is January 25. Just before his birthday, I broke my tooth. I flew into town and left the kids home except for Joel, who was nursing. I went to the dentist and had sodium pentothal and had two teeth pulled. I checked in with my teacher friends and got more books for Butch. After spending the night with Barbara and Doug, I flew home the next afternoon. It was a perfect flight. It was dead low tide, so the inlet was still. It was sunset, so the sky was alive with color and all the color was reflected in the water. To see the reflection of the mountains lit by sunset in the water and then see the mountains was beyond beautiful. I wanted to prolong the flight; the pilot wanted to get me on the ground so he could get back to Merrill Field before dark.

After the dentist was paid, I had a little money left over. I bought Jack a birthday present—a case of beer for $3.99. Sometime before the trip to the dentist, Jim had come up to his dad and said, "Split a beer with ya, Daddy." In that moment, we realized it had been quite a while since we had a drink. The case of beer got put under the bed: first so it wouldn't freeze yet would be cold, and second it was out of sight. Each night one beer was opened and shared. That is until February fifteenth, Joel's birthday. Joel didn't exactly know how to handle himself when he found out that there was beer available but not shared until his birthday. That was the last of the case.

JACK

Mike's birthday was January 31. The family had a party with cake and Jell-O. The neighbors came to help him celebrate his sixth birthday. He got gifts like a package of gum, but everyone was happy and had a good time. After the party, when everyone had left, Butch and Mike took one of the candles out and set it up on a stump. Then they loaded Mike's .22 rifle and tried to shoot out the candle from about thirty feet away. They'd take turns loading the little single shot and shooting. They'd both missed the flame, so the next turn was taken from a little closer. Finally, they were so close that the muzzle blast would have blown out the flame. At that moment, Rita and I walked out the front door to walk her trap line. I told the boys to step back, out of the way, and I swung my rifle up and shot out the flame. The boys were duly impressed and let me know it with "oohs" and "wows." Rita's trap line consisted of six traps and took about an hour to cover if no animals had been caught. It gave us a good excuse to get out of the cabin every day. We'd been back at the cabin for a short while and I was cleaning my rifle when Butch came over to me. He looked around to make sure none of his brothers could hear our conversation. Then this wise old eight-year-old said to me, "Daddy, you didn't fool me with that shot. I didn't say anything to my brothers because they were really impressed and I didn't want to mess that up for them."

Well, I'd been a little proud of that shot myself. I said, "Butch, what makes you think I was trying to fool anybody?"

"Well, Daddy, that 30.06 bullet is a lot bigger, goes a lot faster, and you don't have to get it any ways near as close to the flame to blow it out as we do with a .22."

"I hadn't thought of that, Butch. Thank you for not telling your little brothers."

Twelve years later, Butch took his single-shot kid's rifle to a turkey shoot. Every one laughed when he paid his entry fee. They laughed again when he stepped up to take his first shot. He came home with the turkey, two hams and fifty dollars. And along the way, when he was 13, he shot top score at a Boy Scout jamboree. Guess all those A's on school papers paid off.

CHAPTER 31

RITA

Every morning, Mike and Butch walked over to Joel's for morning coffee. Joel would bake biscuits every morning, and then later in the day complain that the kids had eaten his leftover biscuits that he was saving for lunch. Of course he never made extra, or put the leftovers out of sight, or forgot to offer the kids the biscuits.

Later that year, we would get up and find we had moose close by, but they left as soon as someone got up. So we eased across the floor, staying below the windows, over to the window to peek out, because when one walked and got between the front and back windows, the moose saw something and moved on. One morning there was a bull moose on the runway. Being very careful not to disturb the animal, we used binoculars and checked it out. Finally Jack decided it was a bull, not a pregnant cow. It was lightly snowing and there would be no planes flying. We were out of meat. Jack shot the animal from the doorway and it ran down the runway. Of course, about then the sun came out and everyone with an airplane was soon overhead. The pilots had to remove snow from the wings to keep the weight of the snow from damaging the wings. And while at the airport, why not take a short hop? While Jack was dressing out the meat, the boys and I covered up the blood that was showing on the snow. We used shovels to build a pile of snow over the red blot. As fast as we covered the blood, the ravens came and exposed it again. That blood trail stayed on the runway until all the snow melted. The family had meat for the rest of the year. When it got too warm to keep it frozen, I corned it.

We left the head of the moose and the guts at the far end of the runway under some trees. We knew they would be eaten by critters. One day the boys were bored, so Jack sent them to the far end of the runway to check out tracks. They came back and reported seeing moose, coyote, bird, and grizzly bear. Now, we didn't expect grizzly bear. Jack and the boys started for the far end to check out the bear tracks. Yep, we had had a grizzly. He picked up the moose head and carried it off into the brush so he could dine in peace.

People living as we were had to entertain themselves. We played cards and went to visit our neighbors. We played Parcheesi, slightly modified to speed the game up. We used three dice and one always had to have a move. Mike was really good at calling dice. He would look at the board, say, "I need fourteen." and roll fourteen. Joel was very competitive and wanted to beat Mike at Parcheesi, but never made it. Butch regularly beat me at checkers. Pick Up Sticks was another favorite. Most evenings Jack, Joel, and I would play pinochle. Usually Joel won, even though Jack and I kinda played as a team. At ten-thirty or eleven o'clock we would stop, have a peanut butter and jelly sandwich with cocoa, and then Joel would go home and we would go to bed. One night, just as the game started, I took the kitty. It had two aces. I then laid down the other six. With that, Joel stood up, threw down his cards and walked out saying, "She has every f**** ace in the s** deck." Usually he didn't swear but.... We didn't see him for a couple of days.

Roy's wife borrowed our little light plant to do her laundry. Jack took Jim, our three year old, and went over to bring it back to our place so I could do ours. In the clearing in front of the cabin was a cow and calf moose. Laura had not gotten the water all hauled out to dump when Jack got there, so he was hauling buckets of water out to dump for her. This water was going to turn to ice so it had to be dumped where the ice wouldn't cause a problem. In the process Jack slipped, cracked his head, and came inside bleeding. The question asked by Jim was, "What happened, Daddy? Did a moose bite you?" Funny how questions like that hang around for the rest of your life. Whenever a kid got a booboo, someone might ask, "Did a moose bite you?" What a different environment our kids were exposed to.

Seems to me like every February it rained. This meant that the temperature rose above freezing. When we had this type of weather it was called a Chinook. Usually we also had warm winds and rain that lasted for three or four days. This meant lots of icy-covered ground. This year the hill leading into the basement was a sheet of ice. The rainwater ran into the basement and close to the well. We had to protect our water supply from contamination, so Jack dug a hole between the bottom of the hill and the well, about six inches deep and a foot across. One of us, usually Jack, bailed this hole out, sometimes by flashlight, every hour or so as long as the rain came down for the next three days and nights. Getting up all night long is not pleasant, but sometimes one does what one must do. We did manage to keep the surface runoff water out of the well.

CHAPTER 32

JACK

One day in February, a helicopter landed in our clearing and a guy came walking toward our door. I answered the knock and the guy said, "Baldy says you're a surveyor."

"That's right," I answered.

"We need a surveyor for about a month."

"Where'll I be working?"

"Right here. We've set up a camp over at the Armstrong's and we'll be doing a seismograph of the whole Point MacKenzie area."

"When do you want me to start?"

"Right now'd be about right."

"Let me get my gear."

Baldy had been working for them for most of the winter. They needed a surveyor and Baldy told them about me. We were beyond flat broke and suddenly I'm offered a job where I could come home at night. I didn't even ask the guy how much they paid, because it didn't matter. Some money is a heck of a lot better than none.

The crew was camped at the Armstrong's and paying Marcene to cook for them. Cooking was Marcene's favorite pastime. The Armstrongs were hurting for money even worse than we were and Marcene thought she had just died and gone to heaven.

All the seismic trails in our area were done by bulldozers. The trails were laid out by the surveyors pushing ahead of the dozers. When the dozers had enough trail open, the surveyors came through again and set out markers on a given station for the seismic crew. We set a marker every 220 feet. We set a different colored marker at each mile. A geophone was set at each station for two miles. Each was connected to its neighbor by wire. A "doghouse" containing recording equipment was set at the mile marker in the center of the two miles. A hole was drilled somewhere along the line and a dynamite charge was lowered into the hole and set off. The shot creates many vibrations that go deep into the earth until they reach a point of density that bounces the vibratory echo back to the surface. The geophones pick up these echoes and send them to the recorder in the doghouse. The differences in the vibratory echoes were analyzed in trying to pinpoint if there's oil and how deep it is. Putting all the geophones out, tying them into the recorder, drilling the hole, placing the charge, and shooting it is called a "set." After a set is completed, everything is gathered up, moved ahead, redistributed, and the whole process is repeated again. This can go on for many miles. It's hard, rough work and you have to be in darned good shape to handle it.

I wasn't the surveyor; I was the surveyor's assistant. The surveyor was a fellow from Texas. We'd been working together a couple of days and were driving along one of the seismic trails when we came to a short stretch of wind-blown snow. He stopped the pickup and was studying the snow. I said, "Treat it just like you do the sand in west Texas." He nodded and eased out into the middle of the snow and then GUNNED IT! He sank that truck right to the frame! I darned near bled to death from biting my tongue. I couldn't think of any nice way to tell my boss what a total idiot I thought he was. My mama always told me, "If you can't say something nice, don't say anything at all." We both got out of the truck. I finally was able to say, "I'll go see if I can find some help." And I walked off. I wasn't about to dig that jerk out. I figured that, if I found some help, great. If not, I'd sit down somewhere until he came along.

About ten days after I'd started work, the company owner came to me and said, "We're starting a new crew up in the Susitna Valley. We'd like you to go up there. I realize this could create some problems for your wife, so we're willing to give you a raise to sweeten the pot." It will be ten days on and four days off.

I told him I'd talk to Rita and give him an answer in the morning. We really needed the money and if I waited for construction season to open, I'd probably be working so many hours I'd never get home. We decided I'd better give it a try. If it got too bad, I could always quit. I worked for them for the next seven months. I got transferred to a crew working up at the head of the Susitna Valley. We headquartered in Willow, a wide place in the road on the way to Talkeetna, a wider place at the end of the road. In those days, Willow consisted of a filling station, a trading post, and a few homesteaders. We stayed at the trading post. It was kind of a general store, but it also had a restaurant, a bar, and kind of a bunkhouse affair where we all slept. Each day we flew out to where we were working and each evening we were flown back to Willow. We flew in either a fixed wing aircraft on skis or in a helicopter. Bud Loffstead, who owned Kenai Air Service, flew the fixed wing, and I don't remember the name of the helo pilot. They were both excellent pilots.

A seismograph crew is generally made up of two units: the surveyors, who establish line, elevation, and stationing; and those who do the actual seismology work. I prefer the surveying because we're out in front, kind of pioneering the whole project. It's quieter, closer to nature, and we often get to see things the other guys never get to see. We get dropped off in the morning and set out until it's getting close enough to dark that the plane comes looking for us. It's our responsibility to be near a spot the plane can land and, more importantly, take off with a full load. It usually works.

Our first contract started at the foot of Kahiltna Glacier. We pioneered a line from there southwest to the confluence of Kahiltna River and the Yentna River. We worked each day on snowshoes

146

and cleared the survey trail by hand. It was tough work, but it sure kept us in shape. It also gave us a few adventures.

One day, we discovered a big birch tree that had been blown part way over. These trees have a shallow, but very wide, root system. The tree was leaning enough that the roots on one side had pulled up from their normal place in the ground. The sod and grass over the roots were still intact and the whole thing created a natural cave. There was a hole in the snow back into the cave that had an ice crust all the way around it. That is a classic indicator of a bear den. The hole is a breather hole. The ice is created by the vapor in their breath. Some of us took turns putting an ear to the hole and could hear the bear breathing. The rest took our word for it.

We were working at the very north end of the valley, right below the foot of Mount McKinley. The winter temperatures at the top of that thing can be unbelievably cold. The air up there gets dense and heavy and starts down like an invisible avalanche. It hits the valley floor and spreads out under the warmer air and fills all the low spots. It lays in them until it has a chance to start warming up enough to want to rise, and the whole process starts all over again. This phenomenon is called a temperature inversion, and can be almost a daily occurrence. By mid-March, when the sun is getting far enough above the southern horizon to give warmth, the temperature can go from thirty above during the day to twenty below shortly after dark.

One day, while daytime temps were still between zero and twenty above, we were taking a break and had started a fire. Everybody had dragged in some wood and we had a pretty good fire. Three of us walked down to a site a quarter of a mile away from the fire to set a charge for the seismic crew. One guy fell through the ice. We got him out and started back to the fire. I told him, "You'd better try to run or you're never going to make it!" He didn't believe me and, besides, he was embarrassed and didn't want to give the impression that he was scared. We were about halfway to the fire when he started having trouble. Right then one of our Bush pilots, Bud Lofsted, flew over. He saw the trail of water in the snow behind us and pulled a quick one-eighty, dropped down, and taxied right up to us. We had to beat the ice out of the guy's clothes with our fists so he could bend at the hips and knees enough that we could get him into the plane.

In late April, we were working our way into a range of low hills. The range and the individual hills were well defined and we were cutting our way through a small pass. The clouds had been very low all day and the temperature was fairly warm. There were four of us in the party: Duke, our surveyor; myself; and two brush cutters. I was talking to Duke, our party chief. "These clouds are trapped. They're likely to start really dumping on us so they can lighten up enough to clear the mountains."

He said, "Yeah, we have to either get out of these hills so the plane can find us or start building a camp for the night."

Two things happened while we were talking. The clouds opened up and started dumping flakes that were at least two inches across. The other was one of the guys swung at an overhead branch with his machete. The branch bent. The machete slid along the branch and, before he could stop it, got him on the side of his knee. He was cut right to the bone. Luckily, he didn't sever any blood vessel so there was only capillary bleeding. I told Duke, "We've got an hour and a half to get a lean-to up and get enough firewood in for the night. We better get started." We found a clearing adjacent to a small grove of dead cottonwoods. The first thing we did was build a fire. Next I brought in three small spruce trunks, stuck two down in the snow for uprights, and tied the third one across them for a ridgepole. Duke and I brought in enough spruce poles to complete a frame for our lean-to. Then we brought in the boughs to cover the frame. Duke started cutting and placing spruce tips throughout the lean-to for insulation from the snow. I went to help Billy bring in more firewood. The guy with the cut leg tended the fire. By the time we had everything ready, the fire had melted its way down to the ground. This created a hole about three feet deep, and we scooped out the side between the fire and our lean-to. We stacked more snow around the other three sides. This directed most of the heat toward us. Shortly after we started all this, we heard the helicopter make one pass up the next valley over and one pass back down. That was two more passes than I would have made, given the very limited visibility created by the heavy, wet snow coming down.

We spent a more comfortable night than the pilot. He got completely lost and had to set his chopper down. He sat out the night in a plastic bubble with no heat whatsoever.

We didn't sleep well, but we probably slept better than Joe Rendell, the owner of the company. He'd just sat down to dinner when the phone rang. He was told about a raging snowstorm and that he had four men, a helicopter, and a pilot missing. Not something that would help his food lie easy in his stomach. He spent the evening getting search and rescue operations set up for first light. Then he spent the rest of the night imagining the worst.

The clouds started rising during the night, but they stayed around until just before daylight so the temperature stayed relatively warm. The sun had been up only a short time when Bud Lofsted showed up and soon had another plane land right behind him at the mouth of the little pass we were in. We all headed for Willow Creek Lodge and some food. The chopper landed at Willow at the same time we did, and we all walked in the lodge together. Joe, who had come out of Anchorage in the first of several planes he'd chartered for search and rescue rushed up and practically threw his arms around the chopper pilot, "Man, am I glad to see you!"

"Hey, Joe, we were out there too," I said.

He turned to me in pretended scorn, "Hell, I knew you'd take care of yourself. I had a downed plane to worry about!" Everyone got a laugh at my expense and we all went in to eat.

I mentioned Billy, one of our brush cutters. He was only eighteen. This was his first "man's job." He figured the only thing left to do to complete his rite of passage into manhood was to whip a man. Someone in the crew thought it was funny to point him my way. We ended up walking around each other with our hackles up for two or three days. Finally, one morning he and I were the first ones flown out to where we were going to start the day. The helicopter started back for the other two. We had about forty-five minutes to get this mess settled. I said, "Billy, we need to talk."

"About what?"

"I don't know who is trying to talk you into trying to take me, but I bet he didn't tell you that I have a brown belt in karate."

"I don't believe you."

"Well, it's true. They just want to see the karate because they're curious about it."

"If you know karate, show me some."

"Have you seen pictures of board-breaking demonstrations?"

"Yeah."

"Okay, watch this." I went over to a big spruce tree. There was a branch about eyeball high that was one and a half to two inches thick. That branch was totally frozen and brittle as heck. I knew that if I hit it right at its base so it couldn't bend, it would break. I made a big pretense of total focus and POW! The branch landed about four feet away. I turned to Billy, "Now if that'd been your arm, it wouldn't have come off, but the bone would be broken." His eyes were big as quarters.

"WOW!" By the next day, everybody in camp was my friend. Only one guy in the crew knew the truth. He was our other brush cutter, who had a brown belt in karate.

We finished that job and moved to Granite Point to start another. The Granite Point job didn't throw any big adventures our way, but we did have some excitement. One was our helicopter pilot. He was an ex-military instructor. He was a very good pilot from the standpoint of mechanical skill. His only real problem was that he was nuts. He was an adrenalin junkie. He was always flying right on the edge. I think I was the first to fly with him. We were in a little Bell Helo, just like the ones in the TV program, MASH. Eighty-five mph was its top speed. You could get it up to eighty-eight, but it felt like it was shaking itself to death.

This first day, he and I were scouting out the area of our survey. We spent a couple hours at a thousand feet, getting a feel for the terrain and any routes I could take advantage of that would cut down on having to hack our way through the brush. It was finally time to start back. That's when I found out just what kind of a nut I was flying with. He decided to follow the Ivan River back down to the inlet, and fly the beach back to camp. Well, I love to fly, so I sat back prepared to enjoy the ride. Like all the coastal rivers in Alaska, the Ivan has huge cottonwood trees spaced along the many islands in the river. This idiot dropped down below the treetops and ran a slalom down the river, dodging the trees as he went. At eighty-five mph yet! Damn, it was exciting! At the mouth of the river we turned towards Granite Point.

The company had rented a fishing site for us to live in during this job. It was located on the beach at the foot of a bluff about one hundred and fifty feet high. We flew out over the bluff five hundred feet above the beach. The pilot pulled the power, neutralized the rotor, and let us fall four hundred feet and caught us by cranking in lift on the rotor. He sat the chopper lightly on the beach, and a minute or so later, my stomach caught up with me. We soon had ten men in our crew. The chopper could carry only two passengers. I figured I had a four to one chance that he'd kill somebody else, so I relaxed and enjoyed my rides. It didn't take long before we got rid of that pilot.

151

This contract ran us into spring. Three of us had to walk out an old seismic trail on one of the last days. This was a wide trail created by a bulldozer. It started way up in the foothills of the Alaska Range and ran, straight as a string, clear down to Cook Inlet. We started far up in the mountains and walked about twelve miles to get to a spot where we could be picked up by an aircraft. The snow was gone and the ground hadn't yet started to thaw so, it was easy walking. Here and there, the sun had made the surface a little muddy, but it wasn't too greasy for footing. It did, however, create ideal conditions for leaving footprints. There was a perfectly clear print of a wolf running along ahead of us for almost half of the twelve miles. He always kept a hill between him and us. We never saw him. Each time we crested a hill, there would be tracks showing that he turned around and watched us come over the next hill back. As soon as we got close enough for him to leave, he'd turn and head for the next hilltop. He finally went off into the trees and let us go on by.

I did one more contract with Joe Rendell and his company. It was in the Trading Bay area along the McArthur River. It was full-blown summer by now. The grass was eyeball high and every time we turned around, we were stumbling over bears.

We'd gotten done in the valley and moved our camp up into the mountains and set up in a clearing about an acre in extent. Camp consisted of two Jamesway huts. Jamesways are ideal for a camp that has to be moved often. They're made with a wooden frame and are covered with a canvas quilt. The canvas is two layers with fiberglass insulation between them. One hut was for sleeping and the other for cooking and eating. We dug two pits: one for garbage and one for an outhouse. The outhouse consisted of a hole with a log set over it to sit on. Our food was flown in, packaged in big cardboard egg crates. When these crates were opened up, they gave you a sheet that's four-by-six feet. Eventually our outhouse consisted of a hole, a log, four upright poles stuck in the dirt piled around the hole, and walls on three sides made up of sheets of cardboard. This gave the user a modicum of privacy.

Our trash pit had collected only a few days of offerings when a sow bear with three cubs decided to check it out. We tried a number of ways to discourage her. Nothing worked. Nobody wanted to kill her because of the cubs. We tried to get along and just put up with her.

After about a week of our staying out of her way and her sort of ignoring us, I was sitting on the log one evening. It was ten thirty and dusk. As I was sitting, minding my own business, I noticed the grass moving by the edge of the clearing. Whatever was moving the grass was definitely coming my way. I assumed it was "our sow," heading for the garbage pit twenty-five feet behind me. I made a noise to let her know I was there. I heard a snuffing noise and the grass kept wiggling in my direction. I made another noise and the biggest damned bear I ever saw stood up on his hind legs to have a look. Now, that grass was as tall as my eyes. It came to that bear's belly! I stood up and raised my arms, trying to appear as big as possible. I glanced at the door to the hut. Even with my pants around my ankles, I figured I could make the distance in four or five hops. My second thought was, If I go through that door with my pants around my ankles, I'll never live it down. I'd rather get eaten by the bear! I looked back at the bear and stretched a little taller. He kind of tilted his head over sideways and looked at me as if to say, Don't flatter yourself. You're not worth the trouble. Then he dropped down on all fours and went on around me. I didn't have any trouble finishing what I was there to do, and I got back into the hut as quickly as I could.

The sow and her family were very unusual. Two of her cubs were at least two years old, and possibly three. The third one was a spring cub. This was so rare that several biologists have told me that it was not possible; that the third cub had to be the runt of the litter. The problem with that theory was that this little guy acted like a new cub. He was curious about everything. There was

153

a stream on one side of our camp that was about ankle deep. There was a small cut bank on the other side. One evening mama and her offspring came over the cut bank on their way to our garbage pit. The cubs always walked single file behind mama with Squirt bringing up the rear. This time he spotted a rock shining in the bank. He stopped and looked at the shiny spot. Then he looked at mama, who was still walking on. He looked back at the rock. He looked at mama. The heck with it! He just had to check out that rock! It was calling to him in all its shining glory. He went over and sniffed at it. Nothing. He reached up and touched it. It moved! He dug at it with his claws. It rolled down the bank right at his other paw! He jumped back a bit and the thing stopped. He sniffed at it again. Still nothing. He looked back at the bank and there were more rocks. He dug at couple more and they rolled down the bank. Wow! A new game! Enthralling!

Mama and his brothers had been in the garbage some minutes by now and, suddenly she missed Junior. She stood on her hind feet and looked around, and spotted the little guy at his new game. He'd pulled a real "no-no" in not staying in line as he should. Mama started for him with some serious chastising in mind. Junior looked up and saw her coming and knew he was in big trouble. He was right close to a big spruce tree. Mama was about half way to him when he decided the spruce tree was a good idea. Up the tree! By the time Mama got there, he was thirty feet up. She stood up beside the tree and told him to come down. Nope. Mama hauled off and swatted the tree so hard that a slab of bark flew off. Junior went a little higher. She let out a roar that could've been heard for miles. Each time she tore off another slab of bark, he'd go higher. At eleven thirty, when it was too dark to see clearly, the little guy was at the very top of the tree. We all went in and went to bed. The next morning they were gone.

One day in late June we got three college kids from Brown's Academy in San Diego as brush cutters. They were the epitome of "city slickers." I didn't have to tell them which end was the handle, but none of them had ever touched an ax, machete, or chainsaw in their young lives.

We'd been working three or four days and they were getting the hang of things, at least to the point that they weren't much of a danger to themselves or the rest of us. We came to a big tree that just had to come down. I decided it was lesson time. I explained about undercutting and how to control the direction the tree would fall. Then I fired up the chain saw to demonstrate. I cut out the undercut notch and started the uppercut. The center fibers in the tree started popping and the tree groaned and started to go. Just then a big gust of wind hit us and the next thing I knew the tree spun about ninety degrees, coming over backwards. It came off the stump and dropped butt first and landed right on my big toe. Then it fell on over. Luckily, I was able to get my toe out from under it as it tipped and hurl myself backward far enough to keep it from landing on me. I knew I was hurt, but I wasn't about to take my boot off to check it. Everybody was emotionally shattered. They'd never experienced anyone being seriously hurt before.

"Well," I said. "Now that I've shown you what not to do while dropping a tree, let's start on back to where the plane's going to pick us up." We had to walk about six miles. We walked without stopping because we'd forgotten the mosquito dope and if we stopped even for a moment, the whole world disappeared behind a cloud of the pesky little buggers. We were lucky enough that the pilot was flying something out to the seismic crew and saw us walking. He stopped and picked some of us up on his way back to camp. The wounded guy got to go on the first trip. While the cook was getting dinner on the table, I finally got up the nerve to take my boot off. There were bets on if my toe would come with the boot or not. We debated all through dinner whether I should go to town to see a doctor or not. The cook's helper, called a bull cook, just started picking up plates. He suddenly went into an epileptic seizure. He fell to the floor and started to thrash around, completely out of control. Everybody got up and ran! I was down on the floor trying to hold that poor guy and keep my toe out of his way and yelling at those yellow bellies to come back and help. Two guys came back in and we were able to contain most of the thrashing until the bull cook finally came to. Well, that did it. He obviously had to be flown into town and I went with him.

I got to the Doctor's Clinic, (a medical office in Anchorage), and, luckily, there was a doctor and an x-ray technician still there. The x-ray showed that my big toe was broken in three places. Up to now it had hurt, but it hadn't HURT! That was to come about four hours later. It lasted for days! I slept with my foot in a box because the weight of the blanket was more than I could take.

CHAPTER 33

RITA

Life went on pretty much as it had been. Jack worked away from home and I stayed at the cabin. He came in every ten days, bringing groceries and news of the outside. He always had exciting adventures to tell. The kids couldn't wait for the next adventure. We heard about the college kids burning down the outhouse because someone would not come out, and what happened the next day when Jack was in what was left when the bear arrived. We were told of walking through tall grass on a bear trail when the tracks disappeared.

All the Bush pilots who were working for the exploration company knew I was at the cabin alone, so they checked the cabin every time they flew over. Joel and Roy watched over me, also. They cut wood a couple of times, and would come by to start the light plant on laundry day. The light plant was mounted on a couple of two-by-twelves with some blocking in-between, and the guys just put their foot up on the machine to hold the machine still and pulled the rope to start it. I have short legs and couldn't do that, so I talked Butch and Mike into sitting on the machine. Mike was the one closest to the spark plug. He was the one who got shocked. He was the one who refused to help start the machine after that time.

While Jack was working for the oil exploration company, he broke his big toe when a tree he was cutting twisted and landed on the toe. He had to walk out to get to the place where the helicopter could land. He came home for it to heal and Butch made him a wooden sandal to wear. The family went out for an outing in the Weasel. Naturally, the track came off the sprockets. Jack had to work in the cold water of the swamp in a sandal made of wood with rags to tie it on his foot with the broken toe.

We used the well as a refrigerator. The water was about thirty-four degrees. We had a bucket hanging from a pulley for hauling up the water. Jello would set and we kept our perishables in that bucket in the cold water when we were not hauling water. We had to keep the bucket upright or those perishables floated out of the bucket and had to be retrieved. Somewhere the family had gotten some fresh goat meat. It floated out of the bucket into the well water and had to be taken out or it would pollute the water. The well was three and a half feet square and thirty feet deep. Jack usually went down if someone had a reason to, and came back up hand-over-hand climbing the rope. With a broken toe this was impossible so I was elected. First, I have claustrophobia and second, no way was I strong enough to go hand over hand to get back up the rope. So the two of us rigged a sling and tied it off to the Weasel. I went down sitting in the sling, always looking up at the only daylight available and a light bulb on an extension cord hanging over the center of the well. I fished out the meat and then Jack pulled me up. I can remember looking straight up at the underside of the floor joist and talking to myself. You can breathe. You can make it. You're almost there. Then the knot slipped and I dropped a couple of inches. I flew the last foot or so out of the well.

The water was so cold that when one made Kool-Aid using the water fresh from the well, it hurt ones teeth. I would fill the washer and the two laundry tubs, taking a couple of days to haul the water into the house. I did the laundry in cold water, and even after a few days of sitting, it was still so cold I needed a stick to fish the clothes out to run them through the wringer. I usually emptied the tubs and washer in one day. I still don't know why we never hooked up a hose and used it to drain the water.

We used the light plant to run the washer. While the light plant was running, Jack would shave and I would make angel food cake. In the winter, we had clotheslines all over inside so we could hang all the laundry and then we would crank up the heat and dry everything ASAP. We tried to keep laundry to a minimum. The boys had three pairs of pants. When one got wet out playing, they were hung to dry and then they could be worn again. The same was true for shirts. Underwear and socks got changed daily. We figured out a winter boot for the kids. Galoshes didn't keep feet warm, but didn't let shoes get wet either. We would have the kids put on a nylon sock, then two or three wool socks that had shrunk in the wash, and then the waterproof galoshes minus the shoes. Worked great. Of course, no one wears galoshes today, but moon boots were close to what we used.

Once spring came, clothes would dry outside, so instead of using the inside lines, Jack strung some clotheslines for me. He put some nails into three trees to hold up ropes that were strung between the trees. Joel was less than a year old so he was still in diapers. I pretty much knew how many days the supply of clean diapers would last. Two or three days before he would be out, we started to fill the washing machine and the double laundry tubs. We had two reasons for this: the water had a chance to warm up from its thirty-two and a half degrees, and we wouldn't run the well dry. Besides, pulling all that water up and carrying it inside was hard work.

The day I wanted to wash someone had to start the light plant. It was a small one-kilowatt unit mounted on two-by-twelves. Once I had power, I washed the clothes in an Easy washer with a ringer. Next I could rinse the soap out using the two tubs. Somewhere in the middle, the second rinse became the first, and the first was dumped and refilled with clean water.

While clothes were being washed, I hung the first loads out to dry. Washing took most of the day. One day I was busy hanging clothes when Roy arrived. He was carrying a .22 rifle. One never knew when one might kick up spruce hens or rabbits, so having a rifle really didn't register.

Roy loved to tease and seemed to really enjoy teasing me. Also, he was a lousy shot. He went inside and discussed something important with Jack. Both of them came out the door as I headed inside for another load of wash. As I got to the door, Roy raised his rifle to his shoulder. The next thing I knew, he fired the damn thing. I'm sure he meant to hit a clothespin. Two items of clothing would have been left blowing in the breeze, but he missed. He hit the clothesline instead and dropped the whole line of clothing into the dirt. Before I could say a word, Roy quickly disappeared into the trees. He stayed away for a few days to give me time to cool off.

It was raining and the kids were bored with being indoors all day. I had read to them and played cards, but they were still inside. Finally, I found a piece of leftover shiplap about three feet long. Shiplap was lumber cut to lap over the previous piece with a quarter inch lip and Jack had used it for the floor and the roof of the cabin. It was easier to get into the cabin than plywood. I got down Butch's .22 rifle and laid it on the shiplap with the top of the barrel against the lip. I traced around the gun and then cut the gun out. All I had was a firewood cutting saw called a Swede saw, so it was a very rough job of cutting. I used a drill to make a trigger opening. I only remember making one, so there had to be another gun of some sort for the games played to involve both Mike and Butch. That toy lasted for a long time and when, as a man, Butch wanted to get a special toy for a kid, he would make them a wooden rifle. His were beautiful.

Sometime that spring, Joel drove to the cabins. He came down the beach and across the swamp. This was a major accomplishment. There were at least three creeks he had to cross. No one knows how many times he got stuck. The kids and I were the only ones home at the Stout's. Joel came over to celebrate. He brought candy for the kids. Baby Joel was in his highchair and was given a Jolly Rancher cinnamon stick. He would suck on it, then take it out of his mouth to blow, then suck it again. The kid thought it was great.

For the period of time before Joel went back to work, he would come over every morning for coffee. He left his place, walked a big half-circle checking for bears, had two cups of coffee while complaining about the size of the coffeepot and that there was never any leftover coffee, and then walked a different way home. In the afternoon this was repeated, but a different trail was walked. No bear trouble that summer. My coffeepot was a two-cup percolator because I like fresh coffee. Joel had a large pot. He would make coffee in the morning and keep at it all day. Of course, by dinner it was tar.

Close to the cabin, in the bands of trees left after the clearing, there were a lot of standing trees that were dead, so we gathered these trees for firewood. They make great fires because they are easy to ignite and leave very little ash. We used this wood for warming up the cabin in the morning and for campfires outside in the evening for baked potatoes, hot dogs, and marshmallows. The only problem with this wood was that it was almost impossible to saw into pieces. It was light so I could pick up a tree and bring it down to break it, or lay a tree over two logs and jump on it to break it, but cut it up with either an ax or the Swede saw—no.

Joel was the only adult I saw many days. One day we were going to take the kids into town. We walked over to his cabin and across the swamp to Roy's, and then down to the boat. We went this way because it was about one-half mile shorter and, once the ditch was in, was dry enough to walk. Joel carried our Joel, but Jim insisted upon walking. When we got to the swamp, Joel carried Jim and I carried the baby. I'm sure that Joel was glad that evening that he had never married and didn't have to get others to town often.

When we got to Roy's, Roy's wife promised to make Joel a birth-day cake when he got back from town. I knew his birthday was in February and it was now June. Turned out he proclaimed the fifteenth of every month as his birthday. Until I opened my big mouth Laura forgot she had made him a cake the month before, so she had made him another one.

Jack was on break when we got back to the cabin a couple of days later. We went over to Joel's for coffee. Jim wanted to be on his own, not holding my hand or even staying close to me. He walked alone through the woods, trying to whistle. Jim thought that if Mike and Butch could do it, so could he. Every time we stopped to wait for him or look back to check on him, he got indignant.

Jimmy decided he would go visiting again the next day. When we checked the sand pile and Jim was not there and no one knew where he was, we went looking for him. Finally Jack heard this loud roar of anger, more like a bull moose than a three-year-old. Jim was found because people were able to follow the sound. He was down at the edge of the swamp, stuck in the mud up to the top of his breakup boots. He always knew that he could do anything anyone else did and he was going to visit Joel, except he was using the winter trail instead of the summer one that stayed on high ground. To see a three-year-old stuck in mud almost to his knees, with his head back, turning the air blue is quite a sight. Lucky we found him when we did. If he had fallen face first, the water was deep enough he would have drowned because he would not have been able to get up.

Once spring arrived, I set out a work schedule for us. Every morning we all went out and picked sticks on the runway. Some were stubs left by the cat when clearing. Others were still attached to roots. Either way, they had to be removed. We pulled up small trees, cut off larger ones, and got all the pieces off the runway so a propeller would not kick them up in the prop wash and cause a problem. We worked one hour. The rest of the day the boys were free to play.

After the baby's nap, I took him out back to the sand hill. The older boys were playing in the sand with little cars. I helped with a few sand castles and then I spent another hour throwing sand against the back wall of the cabin. I used a shovel. I would pick up about a quarter of a shovelful and drop it against the back wall. All this hard work had wonderful results. We didn't get so bored because we had something important to do. We used up two of the twenty-four hours and, when I went back to town, I weighed one hundred twenty-two pounds and was wearing the smallest size I had ever worn.

Mike *Joel*

Summer of 1961. Working on runway clearing off excess stumps, etc.

Rita, Jim, and Jet. Only suntan I ever got in my life!

163

Our dog, Jet, was a cocker with 13 grand champions on his papers but he was the runt of the litter so became a pet rather than a show dog. He treed four bears that we know about. Joe Reddington once told Jack that Reddington's dad had used cockers to hunt bears because the cockers didn't get hung up in the alder.

An old freight pallet and some birch poles made a good "homestead" playpen

Butch–eight years old in 1961

Jimmy–three years old in 1961

Time out for some fun while working on the runway. The dog loved plastic lemons and limes.

Mike–six years old in 1961

CHAPTER 34

RITA

When one homesteads federal government land, he is awarded a patent instead of a deed. Until one gets that patent, the land is still government land. To obtain the patent, there is paperwork. Along with a description of what and when, there are witnesses needed. Because everyone started homesteading about the same time, everyone did their paperwork or applied for patent about the same time and we all were witnesses for each other.

We were home the day the inspector from the BLM arrived to check out our application for patent. He had flown in by helicopter and walked all over the area, doing all the inspections in one day. He noticed the garden, measured the clearing, checked that there was an outhouse, a source of water, and a garbage pit—all signs that the family had been living on the land. After a cup of coffee and some homemade cookies, Jack and he left to check out the other homesteads. Most of the time there was no one on the homestead when these inspections were done. Joel's place obviously had been lived on, but I had never seen our neighbors on the other side as long as I was there. They were there the year before we moved on. Because we had all started homesteading about the same time, this inspection covered everyone. The guy had a busy day. He landed via helicopter on the point and walked ten miles or so through swamps and on game trails to get back to where the helicopter could pick him up. We felt it was only a matter of time now until the land was ours.

Before we went to the cabin the first time, I asked the doctor what to do if the kids got sick. Butch had been really sick when he was three and four with throat infections, and we wanted him to stay well. The doctor's words were, "Take a fifth of whiskey and a bottle of aspirin, and if you can't take care of the problem with that, he needs to be in the hospital anyway." Once we got our kids away from other infected kids, our boys were healthy. They played outdoors all winter, came in and got dry and warm, and then went out again.

Jim got bronchitis that summer. The first time he had bronchitis we were in town. After two weeks of coughing so hard that he got up every morning about four and therefore got everyone else up, the doctor gave Jim phenobarbital so the rest of us could get some sleep. I had no way to get him to a doctor from the cabin except to flag down a helicopter. I had to use what I had on hand. I knew rose hips were the basis for vitamin C tablets and believed vitamin C helped prevent colds and therefore coughs, so I went out into the yard and picked a half-gallon of rose hips from the wild roses that grew everywhere. Rose hips are the button or bulb where the flower blossom leaves are attached to the stem, and where the seeds develop. I cooked them and made a juice like one would use for jelly. I strained the mess through a clean diaper. I put everything I could think of into my potion that I had to make the juice taste better. I fed this potion to Jim all day. I have no way of knowing how many units of vitamin C he got that day, but the next day the bronchitis was gone.

Mike also got sick with the symptoms of a strep throat. We got word to town and the doctor wrote a prescription for oral penicillin. Jack's dad packaged the bottle in a small, well-padded box, tied all kinds of colored plastic tape onto it, and had a pilot flying over on his way somewhere else drop the stuff for me. Even with the tape it was hard to find in the deep grass, but find it we did, and Mike got well.

When people get messages dropped from a light plane, the message is placed inside the paper tube of an open roll of toilet paper. As the roll falls it leaves a long tail, making the message easier to find. Years later Joel had company at his place on a Sunday. The plane buzzed the cabin and circled, giving him time to come outside. His Sunday newspaper was being delivered, much to the surprise of his houseguest. The bright plastic wrapper made it easy to find. The visitor was really impressed that a paper boy would use an airplane to deliver the paper.

The rest of the summer the kids played, I read to them, and at the end of August we moved back to town. The people in the house had moved and Jack's folks had moved in. They were going to stay until winter and then go back to Sutton, so they only needed shelter for a little while. I went back to work; Mike and Butch went back to school.

CHAPTER 35

RITA

Somewhere in that winter, we found out that a protest was filed against our draining of the swamp to meet the clearing requirement. The BLM said it was a vandalistic protest and threw it out.

Next came a phone call from the person doing the paperwork for our patent. Early in the process, we had written a letter to the BLM requesting clarification on requirements. Rather than answering the questions, the BLM had sent a copy of the Homestead Act of 1862. We believed that, while maybe not the normal way, we had met all the requirements. The gal on the phone would say you were to do so and so. I would reply, "But that isn't what the law says. It said you may do so and so."

After three or more phone calls, the BLM gal said, "Mrs. Stout, would you have your husband come into the office?"

Jack went in and went through much the same routine. The people said they would have to have a man from Washington DC come up and adjudicate this matter. When the attorney arrived, he told the locals that Jack was correct. What they were asking for wasn't what the law said.

The BLM clerk asked their own attorney, "What do we do now? We have been misinforming people for forty-nine years."

His reply was, "Keep your mouth shut."

Finally, the patent arrived by registered mail and the homestead was ours, or rather Jack's. We sent the patent to Palmer to have it recorded, and Jack's land was added to the tax rolls.

It is hard to describe the feeling of accomplishment, and by God we did it, that came over both Jack and me the first time we went back. We both glowed. We had worked so hard for so long. We had been broke, not hungry but broke, and yet we stayed together, took care of our kids, paid our bills, kept our house, and learned so many things. That night it was hard to sleep because we were so excited. To accomplish something you are not sure you can do is a feeling that everyone ought to experience once in their lifetime.

* * * * * * * * * *

RITA

Many years later a man from the BLM came by Jack's office to talk to him about maps and roads in the Point MacKenzie area. Jack told him there were no roads; some trails through the woods, but nothing anyone could call a road. The guy mentioned being told that there was a road from our cabin to the beach. Jack started to laugh. He looked the man in the eye and told him about pulling down trees with the Jeep and a chain as he wandered through the woods, how he had tried to corduroy the swamp. Then Jack asked, "Would you like to know what my wife named those 'roads'?"

Of course the man said, "Yes."

"One was called Abortion Alley and the other Miscarriage Way."

The man laughed and left.

Epilogue

JACK

Fifty years after our patent there are still no roads in the area. We can drive into the cabin in the middle of winter if the swamp is frozen and the snow not too deep. Currently, we go down a power line right-of-way and across a short cat trail to the clearing. The first trails we used to get to the cabin were seismograph trails put in by the oil companies' exploration in the early sixties. It was twenty-one miles of unimproved cat trails from what was then the end of the road to our cabin. Now in the summer, we can use Honda ATVs to travel through four and a half miles of swamp to the power line right-of-way. Rita and I did the Honda bit in 1982 for the first time. Back then we had to go thirteen miles on the Hondas. At one point we had one machine upside down in a deep puddle with the engine still running. I couldn't get it turned on its wheels first try, so I shut the engine off. BIG MISTAKE! I finally got it turned over and the plug was so fouled that it took me an hour to get the engine running again.

Yes, we still have trouble with bears. Finally, after many break-ins, we put up a solar-powered electric fence around the cabin.

We have added on two rooms and sided the whole thing with plywood.

We have no roads. We have no services. But we have taxes.

RITA

I am now 76 years old and, looking back I realize that I was stupid. No other word for it—ignorant yes, naive yes, but also stupid. We could have looked around, and if we had, we could have done many things differently, but then maybe we wouldn't be who we are today. I am sure I could have stayed in town to work while Jack spent time "across the way" and we would have been in residence, especially if one of the kids was with him. All the time he was building the cabin and sleeping somewhere else he was "in residence," but we didn't count that time either. Guess I should have decided "to hell with togetherness" a lot sooner in life.

We still have one hundred thirty-eight acres of the original one hundred sixty. The power company has five major lines down one side and took the rest of the land for that.

Politicians are still fighting about the causeway between Anchorage and Point MacKenzie. Now some call it the Bridge to Nowhere. The Armstrongs came back to town about the same time we did. Living off the land is almost impossible without some money coming in. I believe they went back to the Midwest. Baldy lives in Kenai and is still a good buddy. Joel is here in town in an assisted living facility.

People claim Anchorage is only twenty minutes from Alaska and happiness is Anchorage in your rearview mirror. The homestead has been our "Anchorage in the rearview mirror" for all of us for all these years. Our grandsons went "Outside" to school. When they would come back, they weren't "home" until they'd spent a night at the homestead. When we're there, we're home. When we're leaving, we fight the urge to load the wood stove as though we'll be back before it burns out.

Our boys, both sons and grandsons, have used the cabin as a sanctum sanctorum. It takes a while to get there, but it is peaceful. Before the boys get serious over a young lady, she is invited to the cabin. If she complains, that's the end of that romance.

People ask us why did you go homesteading. I can't really answer that question. It was a way to get title to land is one reason, but the chance to live away from town on one's own has to play a part. Jack's grandfather getting a start as an entrepreneur by working with homesteaders in Kansas plays another part. Just because it was the fad that year must have played another part.

The next question is why did you go back the second time. That answer is easier. We had no money coming in and didn't want to lose what we had gained in life. We were both depression babies and had watched our parents struggle because they didn't have enough money saved for their rainy day. The homestead was our umbrella.

It's funny to me that people leave work they are paid to do to fight their way to the cabin to do work, usually harder work, for the joy of working. Cutting wood, digging wells, running loaders, clearing snow are all favorite pastimes. Mowing the runway is fun, mowing the lawn is a chore. Go figure.

Inside of cabin today—grandson Michael cooking a meal. Some of the cabinets are still gas boxes. The tea kettles on the wood stove are still our source of hot water.

Big swamp today that we corduroyed years ago. Power poles belong to Chugach Electric and bring power from Beluga to the substation on the point. They go down our quarter section line.

Winter trail into clearing of cabin

THE HOMESTEAD TODAY

Side and back of cabin—no snowmobiles in the old days!

Typical outbuildings on a decades-old homestead

John (Butch) in back of cabin. We used icicles for bath water and for making ice cream.

We have eagles on our property

If we only had ATVs in the old days!

Jack offloading ATV at end of the road, ready for a run into cabin

Rita ready for trip back to Anchorage.
Note electric wire around cabin to prevent bear break-ins.

ATV tracks through swamp...but you can still get stuck!!!

Jack hooking up the "bear fence"

JACK

While working up the highway and staying at Meekin's Lodge, I had the fantastic luck of meeting a wonderful, wonderful old man named Charles E. Gillham. He was in his mid- to late- sixties when we met. He was "making his last run at Alaska." His plan was to run the Stikeen River in a canoe and then a two- week hunt with Austin Meekin. He made most of the river run and then tipped over the canoe. He got wrapped around a rock backwards and was badly bruised.

By the time he got to Austin's, it was obvious that he couldn't last two weeks on a horse. I spent every moment I could of that two weeks visiting with Charlie. We talked about his life and his writings and my life and my writings-yet-to-be. One evening in the bar, Charlie and I had knocked back a few when he said, "Forty years I've wandered Alaska looking for a 'He-Man-of-the-North.' I haven't seen one yet!" I guess he never looked in the mirror. By the time he left, a seed had been planted in my mind. Only God knew when it would start to grow. These poems of Charlie's speak of the Alaska we have come to know and love. They come from his 1950s book, *Sled Dog and Other Poems of the North*.

When the Salmon Run

I've been a long time in this country
God knows it wasn't all fun—
But I always felt like a million,
In the Spring—when the salmon run.

So give me a spot in Alaska,
And give me my gold pan and gun,
I'll half freeze and starve, but it's worth it.
For the Spring—when the salmon run.

Though my hair is white and I totter,
And my long race with life is won—
God, see me through one more winter—
Into Spring—when the salmon run.

Charles E. Gillham

179

Waiting for the Plane

Sitting on a mud flat
Staring in the rain,
List'ning for a motor
Waiting for the plane.

Damn that lousy pilot,
Last week he said he'd come,
Prob'ly drunk in Bethel,
That dirty low-down bum.

He's got grub a-plenty,
Guess his bed is warm.
Folks there he can talk to
While waiting out the storm.

There I hear a motor—
Hell, it's just a kicker:
Some good Siwash brother
Running by with licker.

God, this country's lonesome,
A day seems like a year,
How I'd like a T-bone,
Clean clothes—and a beer.

There I hear a buzzin'
That must be the plane—
Guess I'm getting balmy,
It's only wind—and rain.

Sure he knows I'm stranded,
Can't walk or swim—must fly.
Miles and miles of tundra
He gets me—or I die.

Hunting a bonanza –
Hell, I know it's dumb.
Bet sometime I'll hit it—
Why don't that pilot come?

Grub sack, it's plumb empty.
When have I had a smoke?
Nuggets in my pocket—
I might as well be broke.

Darn these modern gadgets,
They always leave you flat.
Give me boat or dog team,
A man can go at that.

Maybe something's happened,
I know he ain't forgot.
He told me late last winter,
To meet him at this spot.

Getting dark—another night,
Shiverin' in the rain.
Ears sure are deceivin'—
Still I hear that plane.

My God—am I dreaming?
No—by gosh—that's him!
Knew he wouldn't fail me,
God bless good old Slim.

Goodbye, rain-soaked bedroll,
Stand there, tent and mold.
"Hi Slim—Good to see you—
Yeah, I found some gold."

Look—bright lights a shining,
Who said I'm a bum?
Nuggets in my pocket—
Big Town—here I come!

Charles E. Gillham